Dance of the Chickens

Ben Romero

Cover illustrated by Gabriel S. Romero.

Note for Librarians: a cataloguing record for this book that includes Dewey Decimal Classification and US Library of Congress numbers is available from the Library and Archives of Canada. The complete cataloguing record can be obtained from their online database at:
www.collectionscanada.ca/amicus/index-e.html
ISBN 1-4120-4100-7
Printed in Victoria, BC, Canada

TRAFFORD

Offices in Canada, USA, Ireland, UK and Spain
This book was published *on-demand* in cooperation with Trafford Publishing. On-demand publishing is a unique process and service of making a book available for retail sale to the public taking advantage of on-demand manufacturing and Internet marketing. On-demand publishing includes promotions, retail sales, manufacturing, order fulfilment, accounting and collecting royalties on behalf of the author.
Book sales for North America and international:
Trafford Publishing, 6E–2333 Government St.,
Victoria, BC v8t 4p4 CANADA
phone 250 383 6864 (toll-free 1 888 232 4444)
fax 250 383 6804; email to orders@trafford.com
Book sales in Europe:
Trafford Publishing (uk) Ltd., Enterprise House, Wistaston Road Business Centre, Wistaston Road, Crewe, Cheshire cw2 7rp UNITED KINGDOM
phone 01270 251 396 (local rate 0845 230 9601)
facsimile 01270 254 983; orders.uk@trafford.com
Order online at:
www.trafford.com/robots/04-1907.html

10 9 8 7 6 5 4 3 2 1

DANCE OF THE CHICKENS: AN ANTHOLOGY OF LIGHT-HEARTED STORIES
by Ben Romero

INTRODUCTION

Everybody has a story. And every story has a lesson. He who tells his tale, enriches his very self, for sharing is reliving. This book is filled with true adventures and mishaps experienced by people from many walks of life. The material within the pages is meant to be enjoyed with open minds and hearts. Let go your daily burdens and allow yourself a moment in time to graze on life's unexpected. This book is dedicated to my grandchildren; my nephew, Vincent Vigil; and to all the people who contributed stories.

ACKNOWLEDGEMENTS

Special thanks to my parents, Manuél and Delia Romero for their unconditional love, and for instilling in me the desire to pursue my dreams.

Many individuals contributed to this book. Each is an author in his or her own right. My thanks to every single one, beginning with my wife, Evelyn Romero, who has been patient and supportive during writing of my other three books. My children, Pedro A. Romero, Victoria Anna Romero-Delsid, Gabriel S. Romero, Rebecca E. Romero, and Olivia V. Romero wrote at least one story each. My siblings, Ramona Roybal, Virginia Herrera, Eluid M. Romero, Marcella Haber, Johnny L. Romero, and Joseph L. Romero shared experiences. My mother, Delia Romero, and my father, José Manuél Romero added stories. Other authors include Linda Horton, Janet Stutzman, Kenna Morris, Ralph Schleich, Margretta Schleich, Dorothy "Dot" Morris, Evelyn Butler, Heidi Thompson, Rose Brace, Gloria Prine, Berta Guerra, Tom Wilkes, Richard G. Flores, Sr., Harry Young, Nancy C. Ray, Gina Shaw, Peter H. Deutsch, Robert D. Nicoletti, George Vasquez, Connie E. Curry, Priscilla Flores, Kathleen Vigil, Esther Pérez Martín, Lupe Sánchez Garcia, Sandy Chabot, Dorothy Plummer, Serina Galvez, Linda Vonk, Veronica Franco-Cook, Rebecca Rodriguez, Kathy McWilliams, Claudia E. Sonia-Delgado, Lisa Fibietti, Chong Erskine, Shirley Clements, Lila Pacheco, Mr. Bear, Dick Gallagher, Peter J. Rondero, Javier Lazo, David Rodriguez, Tomothy Avid, Christine Jahn, Laura Gibson, and Teresa Navarette.

TABLE OF CONTENTS

iii

DANCE OF THE CHICKENS

By Ben Romero
Dedicated to my son, Gabriel Romero

"Why are you wearing baloney on your head?"

My son, Gabriel was two and half years old. He loved to eat baloney slices without bread. But every time he took some outside our dog would take it out of his hands. He thought he could keep it safe by putting it on his head.

"I'll keep the dog away from you so you can eat in peace," I offered.

I put Chivito in the front yard and closed the gate so he wouldn't bother my son anymore. But when I returned to the back, Gabriel had a slice of baloney on his head again. He was backing away from our two large geese, who wanted a handout.

I picked up a long stick and chased the geese. "Get away from him, you feathery pests," I said.

Gabriel got closer to the henhouse, the baloney slice still on his head. Our old red cat sat on a post, reached a paw down to the baloney, and hooked it off his head. Gabriel looked up in disbelief, tears in his eyes.

"Let him have it," I said with a sigh. "You should just eat inside."

A few minutes later, Gabriel was back outside with a slice of baloney on his head. This time he outran the geese and dodged the cat. He opened the door to the henhouse and stepped in. Immediately, he was surrounded by chickens. They'd get close and Gabe would try to catch them.

Our fearless rooster fluffed his feathers and stood his ground. Then he did a little cocky dance around my son. Gabe was not afraid of chickens and certainly not intimidated by the rooster. He ripped a small piece of baloney and threw it. Dust and feathers flew everywhere as hens fought for a chance at the meat.

The rooster flapped its wings against Gabriel's legs and

resumed his dance. Gabriel jumped back in surprise, then tried to imitate the bird dance. It was a battle of wills. The rooster would advance and Gabe would swing the baloney, causing the rooster to back up. My laughter encouraged Gabe to continue, but like a good parent, I feared for his safety.

"Come out of there before that rooster pokes out your eyes," I warned. Gabe turned to face me and the rooster jumped, snatching the precious baloney. Perhaps it was my fault for distracting him.

I tried to soothe the tears that followed, but as luck would have it, we were out of baloney.

LIFE IN A BASKET

By Linda Horton
Dedicated to my grandkids

I was six years old before I knew some people watered their grass on purpose. I don't know whether I'd ever seen a real lawn before that day. We never went anywhere except Market Square, twice a month to buy supplies. Maybe it was just that there was so much of it at the Greenville City Park where Mama and Daddy took me that Easter Sunday for the annual egg hunt.

That place was the most beautiful thing I'd ever seen; acres of lush green grass, giant shade trees, a large man-made pond where serene ducks paddled about, and swings and merry-go-rounds and seesaws. . . I'd never seen anything like it. I was convinced this was the Garden Of Eden from the Bible that Mama talked about. I'd never seen that many people in one place either. Everyone kids and grownups alike, with faces scrubbed and hair slicked down, was wearing their Sunday-best.

I had on my new dress that Mama had just made out of print flour sacks. I even had my shoes on. Plus, we'd all taken a bath in the big galvanized tub the night before. Me first, then Mama, and Daddy was last. Afterward they lugged the tub out the back door to dump it. That was the extent of our watering anything—Saturday night bath water with a liberal dose of lye soap.

That morning when we stepped out of Daddy's old Ford and got a whiff of that fresh-cut grass I nearly swooned. The only thing that even came close to that smell was newly mowed hay.

We tramped across to where a big group of people were standing in front of a makeshift stage. I wanted to keep going, let my eyes drink in all that greenery but we couldn't. Ribbons had been draped across and tied to trees, roping off a large portion. On the other side of the ribbons, shrubs and flowers were planted here and there. I heard one red-headed, freckle-faced kid to my left whisper to his buddy, "That's where you'll find the most eggs,

3

next to the flowers and bushes."

"Yeah! You take one side and I'll take the other!" They were belly up to the ribbon, Easter baskets at the ready.

I looked down at the brown paper sack in my hand. We'd picked it up at Piggly Wiggly that morning. I didn't feel too bad. I was used to making do. Besides, this was my very first Easter Egg hunt, my first visit to the park, first look at a real lawn, really the most exciting day of my life!

The only thing that would make it better was a sack full of those candy eggs and one of the two-foot-tall chocolate bunnies the man at the microphone had just promised was hidden out there waiting to be found.

Mama squeezed my hand hard so I'd pay attention.

"Listen here, children. They's just a couple a rules. In a few minutes we're gonna cut them ribbons and ya'll will be gathering them eggs to beat Dixie. But we don't want you to run. 'Cause if you do, you're gonna smash the eggs and won't nobody want 'em. And if you're runnin' you're liable to step on another young 'un. So we want you to walk and show your manners and that way everybody'll have a good time. So! Are ya'll ready?"

"Yeah!" chorused the crowd.

"Then line up behind the ribbon over yonder and when you hear this-here pop gun, then. . . git!"

A roar of excitement filled the air and I could feel it coursing through my body.

Mama bent down, still holding my hand.

"Now, Linda Fay, you heard the man. I don't want to see you run, you hear me? I don't care what anybody else does. I expect you to walk. Don't you dare embarrass me!"

She squeezed my hand again, then let go and pushed me lightly toward the other kids who were squeezing up to the ribbon. They were already three rows deep in front of me but I didn't care. I was going to get me some of them eggs and maybe one of them giant chocolate bunnies. I hadn't even seen one, but two feet tall must be pretty big. Why, I'd have enough candy to last me 'til Christmas. Lordy, was I excited!

"On your mark!" the man at the microphone barked.

The kids positioned themselves.

"Get set!"

Every fiber in my body seemed to be screaming, "Get a bunny, get a bunny!"

"Go!" the man squeezed the trigger on the cap pistol and it popped smartly.

The kids took off like they were in a foot race; all running, reaching down and grabbing eggs as fast as their feet could carry them.

I took three running steps before I came to myself and Mama's words thundered through my head, "I expect you to walk. Don't you dare embarrass me."

I glanced quickly around me. The kids were way ahead, still running and grabbing Easter treats. I was all alone a few feet from where the ribbon had been seconds earlier. I turned and searched the crowd for Mama. My eyes met hers. I knew that look well. It meant, "You better mind me, young lady!"

My heart sank and I was fighting back tears as I turned and walked slowly, searching for anything that might have been overlooked by the others. I found two eggs but they had been stomped so badly I didn't even pick them up. I knew there was no hope for a chocolate bunny but I kept walking anyway.

I heard the man at the microphone say, "Look at that little tow-headed girl over there. The only one that ain't running. Ain't that precious?" I knew he was talking about me.

I wiped my tears away so nobody'd see but I didn't feel one bit better. I looked back at Mama who was standing straight and tall, a big wide smile on her face.

I looked back down. My paper sack was empty. My heart was breaking. It didn't help that because of the man at the microphone all the grownups' eyes were on me.

I didn't know it then, but that was a lesson I was to learn over and over in the coming years: those that break the rules are the ones that end up with the full baskets.

*Linda Horton is the author of the inspirational novel, Time & Again, based on a true story, as well as numerous fiction and non-fiction articles and essays featured in magazines and newspapers including Redbook Magazine, Dr. Laura's Perspectives, Lifestyles, Cappers, The Nashville Tennessean, etc. See www.lindahorton.com.

BABY DUCK BLUES

By Linda Horton

There wasn't much for a kid to do in the late '40's and early'50s in rural, north-east Texas where I was born and raised. I was an only child for five years, we had no close neighbors, no TV, and no telephone, and since my father had been "shell-shocked" in the war I had to find ways to occupy my time so that I didn't bother him.

Fortunately we had animals: cows, horses, goats, pigs, dogs, cats, chickens, geese, and ducks. One or more were always having babies and that's who I spent my time with. My mother swore I learned to converse with all of them. I even raised several nests of orphaned sparrows and one of baby squirrels, using an eyedropper to give them food and water.

When they matured it was always difficult to turn them loose but I knew they needed to be with others of their kind. And even though I loved every one, I developed, when I was about four years old, a special affinity for baby ducks, much to my mother's consternation.

At first she tried to ignore it, then she decided it was a passing phase. After awhile she was afraid I was coming down with something sinister and then when it persisted for more than a month she blamed it on a wild gene from my father's side of the family.

The strange spells, later dubbed the "Baby Duck Blues", could happen at any time. I had decided I was going to be a baby duck, my mother would be an ol' mama duck, and we'd live happily ever after in an "ol' rotty house". Mama said I would cry for hours and she would try reasoning with me: "Honey, you can't be a baby duck. Heavenly Father wanted you to be a pretty little girl."

It never worked.

"I don't want to be a little girl! I want to be a baby duck!" I'd rant and rave. Then I'd cry myself to sleep. Mama said she felt so helpless.

Whatever the cause, the spells ended about six months later, probably because my fondness for ducks almost got me killed!

It happened shortly after one of our mama ducks had babies and took them to live in some brush beside the muddy pool where our livestock watered.

Since the pool was inhabited by catfish, perch, snappin' turtles and water moccasins, it wasn't a big surprise when baby ducks started to disappear. After the third abduction, Mama and Daddy decided to catch and pen the rest to keep them out of danger.

They took me with them and put me on the bank in a clearing between some willows and cottonwoods, and told me to stay put. Mama was going in one direction around the pool and Daddy the other, in the hopes of trapping the mama duck between them. If they came my way I was to holler and point them out.

"Okie dokie." I said. And meant it at the time.

But Mama and Daddy'd gotten only half way around when ol' mama duck came half runnin' and half flyin' toward me. I knew they couldn't catch her so in the excitement of the moment I screamed, "I got 'er!" and jumped!

I don't know when it was I remembered I didn't know how to swim, but it was way too late--I can tell you that!

Later, Daddy said he had to go down three times in that deep, muddy water before he finally found me.

I don't remember much about that part of it. But the "Baby Duck Blues" ended as abruptly as they had begun. Mama watched me closely for awhile and only barely flinched when I introduced her to "Gary Lynn", my imaginary friend who lived in a penny match box that I carried everywhere I went. After all, "Gary Lynn" was tame stuff compared to my previous determination to sprout feathers and quack my way through life.

*Linda Horton is the author of the inspirational novel, Time & Again, based on a true story, as well as numerous fiction and non-fiction articles and essays featured in magazines and newspapers including Redbook Magazine, Dr. Laura's Perspectives, Lifestyles, Cappers, The Nashville Tennessean, etc. See www.lindahorton.com.

LITTLE BROWN PRESENT
By Olivia Romero
Dedicated to my brother, Gabriel

Knock, Knock.

"Who's there?"

"It's me. Let me come in and see it."

"Come in," I sighed.

My brother Gabriel ran in my room and reached for Peaches, my pet hamster. I didn't want anyone holding her because it took me a long time to convince my parents I was capable of caring for her and keeping the cage clean. Dad kept saying he didn't want rodents in the house.

"I'm not going to hurt it," said Gabe.

"Okay, here you go."

"Ouch! It bit me." I could hear Gabe complaining as he took my prized pet to show my sister.

"Becca, let me in."

"I'm on the phone. Go away."

"I just want to show you something," persisted Gabriel, my hamster behind his back.

"Okay, but this better be good." She opened the door and Gabriel walked in. I followed close behind. Gabe held Peaches close to my sister's face.

"Eww," said Rebecca, "get it away."

While my brother tormented my sister, the unexpected happened. Peaches left a little brown present on my brother's arm.

"Yuck! Get this rodent away from me."

I took back my hamster, but couldn't help laughing. My sister was back on her phone telling her friends about the surprise.

"You get what you get," I said, "and don't throw a fit!"

* Olivia Romero, twelve, is a seventh grader at Alta Sierra middle school in north-east Fresno. She is active in band and softball. She loves horseback riding and playing her drums. She has three pets: a beta fish, a hamster, and a Chihuahua. She loves to read and is discovering the joy of writing.

SIX STITCHES
By Harry young
Dedicated to my son, Austin Cody Young

One day after I'd arrived at work, I received a phone call from "Holy Family Ed Center" that my eight year old son had fallen and received a "bad and <u>deep</u> cut to the head." My wife had already taken him to the doctor's office, so I drove directly to our pediatrician.

After I opened the door to the exam room, Austin looked up at me from a stainless steel, butcher paper covered table, a pained but toughened look on his proud boyish face. He'd just gotten a crew cut and wore an expression of "innocent boyish majesty".

An hour before, that very morning, he turned and tore out the front door on his way to school. I was struck by how the new haircut painted him as the timeless symbol of boyish youth. The curve of his head was naked, clear and defined, covered with thick bristly stubble begging to be rubbed. Sitting atop his smooth long neck, his little ears at attention on the sides, the tuft of hair made him as irresistible as a stuffed animal.

I thought of his head and face on my way to work and, at the red light, I saw a caricature in the form of a decal in the back window of a large white pick up truck. It was an angry crew-cutted youthful face with eyebrows cocked like the hammer of a .38 police special, and the little fist balled up tight and ready for action beneath the chin. A little snarl of a mouth completed the badge of childish rage. The words under the caricature said "Bad Boy Club."

I thought about how much this brush-cut figure looked like Austin in various stages of outrage, throwing a tantrum. It would have made him mad were I to tell him. He'd think I was making fun of his new haircut.

He knew rage (he got that from me, says my wife); he knew passion. But he also knew love and sharing from a warm and fully

9

feeling heart. Sharing a favorite toy to end a fight with a playmate or lovingly holding a cat in his little Popeye-like arms, he displayed emotion with a totality that could make an adult stop...and remember...and envy.

So there he was with a horrible open gash on the side of his beautiful crew cut head pouring blood, and wondering what lay in store, because it would certainly be more than a Band Aid.

It turned out he hadn't cried at all, even from the moment it had happened, as though he knew he'd need to be strong and hysteria might make things really bad. He could throw such fits over almost nothing that, until this happened, I wouldn't have known he already possessed an inner reservoir of toughness.

As he lay on the table and the doctor gave him several shots prior to the stitching, his little face grimaced intensely, but he didn't make a sound. The stitches came next and it was clear that despite the shots, he could still feel a very odd and discomforting pushing and pulling as the edges of the gaping wound were drawn together to facilitate healing and prevent infection.

When the procedure was completed, Austin looked up at me as we squeezed hands and asked, "Can I get a stuffed animal; can I get a bunny?...It hurt really bad."

A bunny...isn't it what we all hope for down deep, have always hoped for--that love will be the reward for our wounds.

If we learn from our children, perhaps the scars received in the pursuit of love, or fulfillment in general, needn't dampen our spirits.

I thought he was perhaps too weak, too easily rattled; and it was my job to toughen him up for what awaits. I see now, it was my own spirit in need of a boost, which was inspired by the essence of his example. I will remember it for those times my own weary spirit may need to take refuge in its shadow.

*Harry Young is married with two children, Holly and Austin, and is currently serving a life sentence in a federal institution (the US Postal Service). He is a former Marine and a flawed Catholic who fancies himself a karaoke singer. When he sings, he works without a net--no drinks. While he overcame his fear of heights with an 18-story bungee jump in Las Vegas in 1998, he has since developed a fear of widths. If you passed him in the hall and asked, "How's it going?", he'd probably say, "Pretty good, but my standards are low."

10

HOUSE CLIMBING

By Ralph Schleich
Dedicated to my wife, Margretta

Grandpa's old house was a great place to play. It was next door to my father's, so when I went to visit Dad, I played there while both of them worked on the dairy.

A swarm of bees found a home in the wall of the upstairs' bedroom and occupied it for years. They got into the bedroom, but couldn't easily get out. Hundreds would fly around the rooms upstairs. Most died and piled up on the floor. In the heat of summer, honey would run down the outside wall and drip on Grandpa's bedroom window.

One summer, when I was nine, I decided to investigate the honey phenomenon. I couldn't see anything from the ground so I crept upstairs and opened the window. Didn't see much, so I crawled on to one of the support beams. Most of the porch roof was gone. During the summer, I went barefoot and without a shirt. In no time the bees were all over me. I knew to stay still, but this didn't do any good. I began to inch back to the window. They were in my hair and ears. My stomach was covered. I had to get back in the house, but how?

-If I move, I'll touch some. If one stings, I will jump and then they will all bite. Move slow...slow. I'm goin' to be a gonner.

I'm at the window.

-Don't sweat.

A little breeze. Some leaving.

-Gotta get my butt in the window. Keep slidin' back.

Bees flying everywhere. Still all over me.

-Be careful. Don't squish any. Try to stand. Slow. Look around to see if they leave. Back up. Slow... slow.

I headed for the stairs and took a quick look.

-Can't see any on me!

Flew down stairs. Hit the door. Closed it fast. Looked again.

-I made it!

I went back just before sundown and closed the window. I never sat on the porch roof again. But my love for climbing and my endless curiosity never ended.

In 1942, when I was eleven, I decided to venture up in our old tank house. I knew my aunt and uncle would not want me up there so I had to be quiet.

I had been on the bottom floor many times. To open the door I lifted a bolt from a hinge and pushed. I went down two steps. The concrete floor came up all the way around the outside walls making the foundation. It had one old window to the north and one to the east. Neither of these had been opened or washed in my lifetime. They were stuck tight. A green tinge covered them from the rain and overflowing tank water splashing on them. The glass was uneven and if the light hit just right, a rainbow appeared.

The room had fascinating odors. Dampness, mold dust, apples, pears, meat and things that defied definition blended into a strange but comfortable smell. Sides of beef, pork and sometimes venison had hung in the room. We bought apples and pears in large wooden lugs and stored them on the floor. Pears needed a cool, dark place to ripen and apples would keep all winter.

Wooden shelves lined the west wall from floor to ceiling. All sorts of interesting things were stacked on them, covered with cobwebs and dust. Empty canning jars were on the shelves. Boxes contained left-over garden seeds, rope and twine. Old moonshine jugs were scattered about. Hand tools nestled amongst the jars and boxes. We stored rows of home-canned fruits, jams, jellies, potatoes, carrots and other fruits and vegetables in two large freestanding cupboards with screen doors. They stood on either side of the stairs to the second floor.

I didn't stop to inspect any of this, as I wanted to see what was ahead. The stairs were made of large wooden planks. Each was a different height and all were steep. The third step wobbled. I could see why no one wanted me up there. No wall or railing on the one side. I crawled up. They wound around in a half circle. Cobwebs and spiders were everywhere. At the top, I stuck my head into the room. The three windows made the room bright, as broken panes let in sunlight. I could see where it had rained, staining the wood. There were no shelves or cupboards, only dirt, cobwebs, and broken glass.

I looked around for another stairway. In one corner of the ceiling there was a square hole to the next floor. Under the hole, large boards were nailed to the wall, forming a stationary ladder. I crawled into the second story and crossed to the ladder. I started up. Boards wobbled. I was sure they would break, but I was more curious than afraid. At last, I could get my head through the opening. A huge metal tank filled the room, leaving only a small space in each corner. A short way from the hole was a metal ladder attached to the top of the tank. It resembled the modern day above-ground swimming pool ladder. I climbed once again.

When I got far enough to see into the tank, I was shocked. It was worse than any horse trough. Large hunks of green moss floated on top. I couldn't see too much but imagined all sorts of things, dead and alive in that water.

When I had to take a bath that night, all I could think of was the green stuff.

My curiosity next drew me to my dad's tank house. The next time I visited, I made it a point to investigate it. The bottom floor wasn't as interesting as Uncle Ward's, but there was a gas engine used to pump the water to the house and barn. Part of the machine went through a hole in the outside wall. It had a large cloth belt that turned a wheel. When turned on, the noise was deafening. The building shook and dust flew.

I squared my shoulders and gathered courage. I went up the outside stairs to the second floor and opened the door. It was dark. No windows on this floor. Boards were nailed to the wall for a ladder. Up I went. As I stood up, I banged against the side of the water tank. I heard a flutter sound above. A whole family of barn owls perched on the edge of the tank. They opened their eyes in unison and flapped their wings.

I flew down the ladder missing half the steps. I didn't look back to see if they were as scared as I was.

Although we don't have open water tanks anymore, I still drink very little water.

---

* Ralph Schleich grew up in the 30's, the son of a dairyman. In 1953, he graduated from Sacramento State with a degree in Social Work. After serving in the army, he became a mortician and worked at Jay's Chapel in Madera, California for eight years. He later served as Supervisor for the Madera County Welfare Department for twenty-six years. Ralph writes for pleasure in a style that is pleasant, funny, and easy to read. He also has six grandchildren.

WEEBLE PEOPLE

By Ben Romero
Dedicated to my son, Andy and my daughter, Victoria

I lay on my back, oblivious to the world around me. I had worked overtime the previous night, as usual, and was droopy-eye tired. It was a mid-summer morning, but with shutters over the glass doors and windows my room was dark.

"Zoooooom, zooooom," my five-year old son's high-pitched voice danced about like a mosquito searching for a spot to land.

I felt my four-year old daughter's hot breath on my neck, as she climbed on my bed. "Weeble People," she said, in her clear, precise voice.

My eyes fluttered open for a moment and I saw my son swooping the large toy airplane inches above my face. "Zoooooom."

"Weeble People," repeated Victoria.

"Take the Weeble People plane in your room to play," I said. "Daddy needs to sleep."

"Look, Dad," said Andy, swooping the plane on my stomach for a landing. "The Weeble People are in here."

He opened the plane and out plopped the contents: two sandwich bags, each holding a limp baby chick.

I jumped, eyes open wide. "Those aren't Weeble People! You can't put baby chicks in plastic bags." I tore open the bags and placed the poor little birds next to me. "I think they're dead."

"We were just giving them a plane ride," said Andy.

"They're going *mimi* like you," said Victoria.

Not knowing what else to do, I lifted and blew on the chicks. Within a few moments, fuzzy haired wings began to move and tiny toothpick legs twitched and wiggled.

"Oh, look. They're alive." I was glad and angry at the same time. "Don't ever take those chicks from their mama without permission," I growled.

Andy backed away from the bed. Victoria's lower lip puckered.

A stubborn tear appeared but didn't drop. "You said they were mine."

"You're right," I sighed. "I did say when the eggs hatch, the chicks would belong to you. I'm sorry I got angry. Come here, both of you."

With one child on each side of me and two dizzy chicks on my lap I said what I thought they needed to hear. "I wouldn't want somebody putting *my* babies in a plastic bag and riding them in a plane. Would you? I'll bet the mama hen is worried about her babies. Can you understand that?"

"Sorry Dad," said Andy.

Victoria gave me a silent hug that spoke volumes.

"Now, how about taking the chicks back to the nest? Later we'll ride the *real* Weeble People in the plane."

It wasn't until later that day that I understood why they'd placed the chicks in the plane. When I lifted one of the Weeble People, I realized it was shaped like an egg.

WOMAN IN THE ATTIC
By Connie E. Curry
Dedicated to my daughter, Katie

I get myself into the dandiest messes.

It was spring, and yard sale time. I had packed away all those treasures in the attic of our garage, for future sales. My junk is someone else's treasure, as they say. Katie, my youngest child was three.

Being fearful of heights, I prefer my feet on the ground at all times, except when I sleep, of course.

My husband had covered the rafters, making a floor for storage, and it was very practical for hiding away useless items. He built a small entrance door in the middle. With the extension ladder, the entrance looked easy. Heck, I had watched him climb it many times.

The weather was warm and the day early. What a great time to get the yard sale items out and start preparing.

This would be simple. I could climb the ladder. I looked waaaaay up, mustered courage and decided to pretend I was a carpenter and climb up.

Katie was inside, preoccupied with Sesame Street. I thought I could hurry up the ladder, into the attic and start dropping yard sale items.

I could then take Katie outside, start pricing all my bargains, so people could ask a lesser amount. One thing to remember in the garage sale business...people usually will not pay the masking price amount.

I started up, stepping slow and careful. *Don't look down.* I held tight to each rung.

I reached the top. I was elated! My heart started to slow down, and I breathed a sigh of relief. Just as I climbed into the hole, my shoe caught on a rung. I heard the clatter of the ladder as it hit the floor. I was trapped.

I lay on my stomach peering down. The ladder appeared to be as far away as the blue sky. Panic set in and I immediately thought of Katie alone in the house. She was clueless as to where I had sneaked off. Was she safe? Was she watching television? Was she playing in the toilet, or trying to bake cookies? Was she climbing up on the kitchen counter because her unfit mother had not fed her lunch? Maybe she was dehydrating, needing a drink of water and standing at the sink crying. I thought about jumping, but I feared landing wrong, and possibly breaking my ankle. The wind whirled. Spring winds! How would she hear me? Would she become curious as to where her mom had vanished and come to investigate? I sat, listened and thought.

When it was apparent she was preoccupied and had totally forgotten the woman that had brought her into this world, I panicked and screamed! I inhaled and hollered at the top of my voice. "KATIE! KATIE! COME HERE! I AM IN THE GARAGE!" I called her name, over and over. Just when I thought she was injured, or asleep, she appeared. This child looked like a giant hero when I saw her come in the garage. She would save me.

"Up here, look up, Katie!" Her eyes met mine and she looked at me and did not even seemed puzzled. "Katie, I need your help. Mommy can't get down."

She shrugged her shoulders and stomped her feet. "Mom, I am watching Sesame Street!" She turned and fled.

I was furious. To think of all I had done for that child. I bathe her, clothe her, feed her and trim her toenails. I brush her hair and scratch her back. To think I *even* get up during the night when I hear her cough to give her medicine and to turn on the vaporizer.

I screamed some more. She came in again and this time she looked up and said, "Mom, I'm hungry. I want soup!"

In this circumstance, I would have been thrilled to be in the kitchen, cooking, scrubbing floors or doing anything labor related. To this child it was as simple as 1-2-3. Come down and be a mom!

It was time to reach deep into my memory bank and think about girl scout days and the improvising we did on camp outs. I started looking for something to help get me out of this mess. Sled! I found Katie's cute little duck sled. It had a seat in it. Next, I found a rope. I was in business. All I needed was the telephone and Katie certainly could go find the cordless.

She followed my directions and brought the phone. I tied the rope to the sled, lying on my stomach and slowly dropped the sled down to her. The entire time, she listened and followed my advice.

I made it a game. I did not want my frustrations or fears to show. Besides, she could really take advantage of me in this situation. She could have had a big Crayola party and redesign the walls. She could have decided playing in the Crisco might be fun.

She placed the telephone in the sled and very slowly I started pulling it up. Just as I got it half way, it slid off the sled. It fell about eight feet and slammed onto the cement floor. Certainly, it was destroyed. Now what would I do? Katie could not go in, dial a number that I rattled off to her. A three-year-old couldn't remember a seven-digit number from memory. They hardly can dial a phone, can they? 9-1-1 was not even a choice. This was not a life-threatening emergency, I was just temporarily stupid.

Just as I grew bleak and tired of trying to entertain Katie in efforts to keep her near me, and safe, the telephone rang. It worked! I told Katie rapidly, "Answer it, hurry, push the button, and turn it on."

Please don't hang up, I prayed silently on the fifth ring. Katie mastered the on button and as quickly as I saw her put the phone to her little ear, I hollered, "Help, I am not hurt, don't call 9-1-1. Just help. I'm trapped!"

I hoped my voice was heard.

Jed, our contractor and friend saved me that day. He was miles away and unsure what my emergency was. He called Gene, the next-door neighbor.

Oh, I was not going to bleed to death, die of hypothermia or dehydration. However, my pride was hurt deeply. Gene, our kind elderly neighbor sympathized with me. He picked the ladder up, held it as I shook, going down the steps. I am sure he wanted to laugh. I knew there was good reason why I always feared ladders. They move!

Katie was not scarred for life internally or externally. It was some silly, stupid game to her. I saw Jed recently and to this day he teases me and we laugh. Years have gone by, and I will never climb that darn ladder again. I suppose if my child or pet were trapped, I would venture up a ladder, but next time, I'm taking lunch, a potty and the telephone with me.

*Connie E. Curry is a Freelance Writer in Delaware, Ohio. She spends much time writing humorous nonfiction stories. In July 2001, she won the James Thurber Humor Writing Contest. Her story, WET DREAMS is a nonfiction about her son. Visit her website at http://www.geocities.com/conniescorner04.

BAD-HAIR DAY

By Ramona Roybal
Dedicated to my sister, Marcella Haber

It was the late '60's. My parents had moved from New Mexico to San Jose, California. Along with them were my sister, Marcella, and brothers, Louie, Benny, Johnny and Joseph. Virginia, another sister, lived nearby in Santa Clara, California, with her husband and two children. My husband, Leroy, and I had jobs with a government subcontractor in Los Alamos and remained in New Mexico.

As was our custom, whenever we took a vacation, we drove to California to visit the family and enjoy the beaches, ball games and tourist attractions. During this particular trip, Marcella was a teenager. The latest fad among young girls was having long, straight hair. Marcella had long dark, curly hair.

Our dad had been to the barbershop that week and had told the barber about Marcella wanting to straighten her hair. The barber sold a hair straightening product to our father and gave him instructions on how to apply the product and how long to leave it on.

Marcella was excited at the prospect of having long straight hair like her friends. We decided that I would apply it for her and time it as Dad had instructed us.

"Don't do it," Leroy warned over and over.

But I argued that if it was sold in a barber shop, it should be safe and effective. Also, I knew what it meant to Marcella to look like her friends.

So I applied the product and ran the comb through to straighten the strands of hair. Sure enough, when the timer went off, Marcella had long straight hair. Now it was time to rinse off the straightening solution. We were all excited to see how she would look when she was done drying and styling her hair.

Leroy and I were scheduled to return to New Mexico the next day, so we went about our business of packing our bags and getting ready for our trip back.

I was still packing when I turned and saw Marcella standing at the door. Her eyes were big and round. In her hand she held a hair brush with a lot of long straight hair. I felt an immediate knot forming in my stomach as she told me that her hair was falling off. I was too stunned to cry. *What have I done?*

The entire family was in a state of shock as more and more strands of hair fell off. I don't think anybody slept that night. I prayed an entire novena to St. Jude, the patron saint of hopeless cases.

Naturally curly hair runs in the family. Dad said he was glad he hadn't tried the product first. He said he would call the barber, but this was Saturday night and the barber shop was closed on Sunday and Monday.

Leroy and I left the next day as planned. I had a heavy heart as we traveled. Part of me wanted to know what the barber would say; the other part of me was in no hurry to find out.

Like it or not, Tuesday came and Marcella went to see the barber. After checking her hair and scalp closely, he told her what was happening. Previously damaged hair was stressed by the straightening solution and was falling off. It looked like a lot because it was long and thick. Within a few days, it quit falling and Marcella had long, dark, straight hair. We could all finally breathe a sigh of relief.

When I think that Marcella could have lost all her hair, I still get a knot in my stomach. Whenever I feel that I'm having a bad-hair day, I stop and remind myself that a bad-hair day is better than a 'no-hair' day, any day!

A VISITOR TO THE CAPITAL
By Peter H. Deutsch, a.k.a. DOC
Dedicated to my daughter, Marion

In 1993, Cathy and I took our two daughters, Natalie and Marion, on a trip East. Natalie and Marion were eleven and ten at the time. We made our way from Virginia to Massachusetts over a three week period.

One drizzly evening, we stood in a long line that snaked around the Washington Monument. With so much to see, we had resigned ourselves to being patient. Our daughters realized that waiting in line was necessary to enjoy all the treasures our nation's capital held.

As people do in D.C., we were all talking with others in line. "Where are you from?" "Have you seen…?" were questions that made the wait more tolerable.

suddenly, we noticed a very tall young man walking towards us and he proceeded to stand next to the people in front of us.

Marion, who couldn't have been over three and a half feet tall at the time, reached up and gently tugged the young man's shirt.

He turned around, and being at least 6' 6", couldn't see anyone, and continued his conversation.

Marion tugged on him again. He turned around and again didn't see anyone.

Marion pulled harder, and when he turned around and looked down, Marion looked up at him and said, "No front cuts!"

He looked from Marion to Cathy and me and blushed. "I'm visiting from Australia," he said. "I hope you don't mind me joining my friends."

Marion let go, and with eyes glaring, said, "OK, but only because you're a visitor to our capital."

*The a.k.a. 'Doc' is a nickname, since P.H.D. are the initials my parents gave me (they had high hopes); I did earn a degree in economics from U.S.F. In 1994, a book I designed and created, giving a thumbnail postal history and current information of every post office in the San Francisco District was accepted and resides in the reference library of the Smithsonian National Postal Museum, and in the Historians office at postal HQ in Washington, D.C. It was the first of its' kind.

GETTING READY FOR THE FUTURE
By Peter H. Deutsch, a.k.a. DOC
Dedicated to my Daughter Natalie

I have always enjoyed cars and from a very young age, I've taken my older daughter, Natalie, to the various car shows that visit Northern California as well as having her accompany me when I want to look at a possible vehicle to purchase. I've told her that a car is more then just transportation: a clean, well maintained automobile can be an extension of you and sends a message to other drivers about what's coming up in the rear view mirror, what just passed you (always safely and courteously) on the left, and what's sitting in your driveway as you wash and wax it to a high sheen. You take care of it and it will take care of you.

When Natalie was 15 and in high school, she reminded me that the San Francisco International Car Show, one of the largest on the west coast, was going to be in town for several days and could we go see the hundreds of new and custom cars?

"Of course," I said. "Do you want to invite any of your friends?"

" No, I talked to them and no one is interested. They're going to the mall. But I definitely want to go."

Having come from a family of only boys, this was a golden opportunity to learn more about the thought process of a female teenager. I asked Natalie why she didn't want to go shopping and she said, "I'll be able to get my license soon and I want to be ready!"

Natalie has a spotless driving record and drives an even cleaner dark blue Jetta with cream interior. Am I proud? You bet!

*Peter H. Deutsch has been part of the Postal Service since Halloween, 1966. During that time he has collected mail, delivered parcels, been a letter carrier, been a training supervisor, worked in labor relations, been an account manager, helped coordinate seven National Postal Forums and currently is the assistant to the District Manager of San Francisco, covering the 157 post offices from Sunnyvale, California to the Oregon border. He loves traveling and drives an immaculate silver Audi TT Coupe with plates: ZOOOMMN. He and his wife, Cathy reside in Burlingame, CA.

VINEYARD

By Priscilla Flores
Dedicated to my parents, Miguel and Alicia Contreras

It was the season of the *pisca,* the time of picking grapes. Vines full of leaves hid the luscious fruit. Farmers were trying to get in the last watering, to increase the sugar content, along with the sun's ripening power. Soon they'd be laying trays to turn grapes into raisins. Rows would have to be flattened to provide a smooth, flat surface. The smell of ripening grapes was sweet.

The day was hot. Beads of sweat ran down our faces. We lived in the country with neighbors to the left, right, and back. It's unusual to live in a rural area and have neighbors so close. It was nice living there. In front of the house were fields with vineyards, intermingled with houses.

On hot days, the other children and I walked alongside rows that were being irrigated. The water would cool and refresh our bodies. Sometimes we sat on the standpipes where the water was released. This was most fun. We held contests to see who could stop the flow by just sitting on it.

Other times we lay on our backs, with the water trickling all around us. We'd lie there being refreshed and imagine that we were in some exotic place. With the sound of water flowing, and the partial sun beating on our little brown bodies and the sweet smell of ripening grapes, it was easy to drift off. We dreamt only happy thoughts. It was also soothing to just sit and let the water ripple on our feet, while we tried to carve figures out of the *terrones* (dirt rock).

I loved to play in the grapevines close to the house. I would look for the perfect spot to sit. The vines would have to be full enough to provide good shade and flat enough so I could sit without feeling those terrones on my behind. Of course there would have to be tasty grapes within reach, so I could have my snack at my beck and call. This was my time to escape in my thoughts. It was soothing to sit and think. It brought me solace.

When I was a baby, my parents used to leave me in the row in front of them during picking season. They could not afford a babysitter. Mom worked hard from morning till mid-afternoon, then she would take the younger children home. The older ones worked all day. Mother would bundle me up and lay a bed for me to sleep or play. She would clean the area so there would be no spiders and just far enough so I would not be in the way. Because of this, I found solace in just sitting under the vines. One hot summer day when I was eight years old, the rancher was close by checking on the water valves. He did not like us playing in his field.

"Get out of here," he yelled.

We found it entertaining to hide from him. Later, when we felt we were out of danger of being discovered we tried to find one another. I now understand that he didn't want us getting hurt. But at the time we considered him a mean old man.

Whenever we knew he was close, we'd duck or crawl into a vine that was nice and full and could conceal us. I remember once hiding in a vine and staying still. I could hear the leaves rustling behind me. My breathing was getting stronger; I knew that I must remain calm, otherwise he would hear me. My heart was pounding from fright. I had never been captured so I didn't know what the consequence would be. *What will he do to me?* I didn't want to find out. Tension grew. He was only a few feet away. I knew my time had come. I tucked myself into a little ball, my feet under, and my head down. *If I come out now, I'm done for.* I just froze, and felt my heart coming out of my throat.

A feeling of relief overcame me when he walked past and continued through the row. He didn't even stop to turn around. He just kept on walking till he got to the end of the row. I guess he thought I had moved on to play elsewhere, or was it that he enjoyed scaring us in our games? I don't know.

After that year, I didn't play in vineyards as much. It was not as much fun anymore. I guess my childhood was leaving me. I started to notice boys, which became more interesting. I guess that is all part of growing up.

MUD AND GRAPES
By Berta Guerra
Dedicated to all my siblings

I could hear Papa getting out of bed and putting on his work clothes and boots. It was still dark outside and my bed was so warm, I dreaded the moment he or Mom would come to my bedroom door and say, "Levántense (get up)."

I hated working in the grape fields. I got up whining and complaining as usual.

"I can't find a pair of jeans to wear. Can I please stay home? I have a headache. My stomach is upset." Nice try, but it didn't do me any good.

Mom made oatmeal and toast. The day before, she made eggs and bacon with hot, fresh tortillas (we never had store bought). This day was not starting well.

We piled into the family car and made our way to the field. The morning star shone from a clear sky. Dusty, cold air hit my face from the open car window, giving me a chill.

By daybreak I was pulling grapevines apart to cut clusters. I felt millions of white flies swarm toward me. They went up my nose, and into my mouth and eyes. I could barely see the grapes, much less cut them. As the day grew hotter, I got sweatier and my hands started perspiring in my rubber gloves. The grape pan felt heavier each time I lifted it to spread grapes on a paper tray to let them dry into the delicious raisins I now love.

"Vamos a comer (let's go eat)." Dad's words were music to my ears. The rancher had a basin for us to wash our hands. We gathered in a circle and got a cool drink. The shade felt good. Mom passed out the burritos she made that morning, and handed Dad a fresh green chile to go with his meal.

After eating, Dad put his hat on his face, lay back, and took a siesta. Instead of resting, my siblings and I played and talked about what we were going to buy with our share of the money.

Too soon, Dad got up, put his hat back on his head and said, "Vámonos (let's go)."

The second half of our day was more miserable than the morning, mostly because of the heat. We hadn't been working ten minutes when I disturbed a beehive near a grape cluster. Before I could react, I got stung on the tip of my nose. I screamed. Papa ran over, fanning the bees away with his hat.

"No te muevas, hijita (don't move, little daughter). With tender arms and calloused hands, he removed the stinger. Then he poured water from his canteen on the dirt and made mud.

All my siblings were around us, but when Papa put the mud on my nose, they started laughing. I must have been a sight, with a big wad of mud on my swollen nose.

The next time Papa said, "Vámonos," it was the end of the day. Hallelujah! We piled into the car for the ride home.

"Dibs on the shower," I yelled.

"Too late," said my sister, Norma. I called it first."

"No way," growled my brother, Jess. I called it before you.

*Berta Guerra is a retired Postal employee, now working in education. She has two children and two granddaughters. She and her family reside in Fresno, California.

DEAD CAT TALES CONTEST

By Dorothy Morris

Dedicated to my sister Erma, a Louisiana resident of 58 years

"My wife's cat had been gone for several days. She'd been fretting about Miss Puss ever since she turned up missing. I kept telling her not to worry, that she'd come back someday. Well, time went on and my old lady kept stewing about that gol'dang cat. One night we wuz eatin' Chinese take-out. I looked at the food on my plate. I sez to my wife, 'Honey, I know what happened to Miss Puss.'" My Louisiana coon-ass nephew hesitated to keep us in suspense.

Then he continued, "My wife sez, 'Have you seen her?'"

He looked at me, then at Raymond, and finally at his mother-in-law, before he went on. "No, I ain't seen your cat. But I seen her eyeball afloatin' on my plate."

I love swapping stories, so I said, "Jerry, I have a real cat tale to tell you. I went out the kitchen door one morning and saw Jan's blue Manx stretched out on the step, deader than a door nail. He must've been hit by a car. I decided to wait until after school to tell her the bad news. I slipped the cat in a plastic department store bag and put it on the floor of the old Ford pickup. After the kids were at school, I headed for the dead animal depository. On the way I remembered I had an errand at the mall. I left the truck unlocked while I ran to make my purchase. I was gone just a few minutes. I threw my purchase on the seat. As I put the key in the ignition, I blinked my eyes and gaped in astonishment. There was nothing on the floor. The cat was gone. Some opportunist walked by, saw the high-end department store bag, reached through the open window, and stole it. I wish I could've seen the thief's face when he opened the bag."

After we had a good laugh, Raymond piped up, "I've got the

29

best tale of all. My neighbors had bought a new Cadillac and were goin' to take their friends out to eat. When they drove out of the garage, they found their cat dead in the street. The man stopped, slipped the pet into a plastic shopping bag, and placed it in the trunk. When he arrived at the restaurant, he parked the Cadillac where he could keep an eye on it. Thinking a dead cat might leave an odor in his new car, he placed the bag under the rear bumper on the pavement."

The two couples went inside, chose a seat near the window, and ordered their food. Twasn't long before they saw a woman pick up the bag and carry it into the restaurant. She put the bag on the floor by her chair and gave her order to the waitress. They kept watching the woman. Sure enough curiosity got the best of her. She peeked in the bag to see what good fortune she possessed. She screamed and fainted on the floor. Someone called 911. Sirens wailed and brakes squealed. Two EMT's ran into the restaurant. They lifted the woman onto a gurney. Then they placed her purse and bag beside her. Not many dead cats get to ride in an ambulance with sirens clearing the way."

Two Louisiana coon asses beat one Hoosier at telling tales.

Dot Morris is a veteran of WW II, a retired elementary school teacher, mother of four, watercolor artist, and storyteller. She met her match in telling tales on a recent visit to Louisiana and wrote this story at the request of her sister. Writing a narrative of her life from a farm girl in southern Indiana through retirement in North Fork, California keeps her young at 82. Dot finds time to teach Bible study at her church.

HONEY, I FIXED THE CAT
By Kathleen Vigil
Dedicated to my son, Vincent and my daughter, Valerie

A year ago, we were having trouble with mice getting into our shed and making a mess. About the same time, a stray cat showed up on our doorstep. We saw her as the most natural mousetrap available so we adopted her as our own. Because of her striped coat, our seven year-old son affectionately named her "Stripey".

I wasn't too keen on the idea of having a cat as a pet. I never had one before and wasn't sure what to do with them. What I did know is that one was enough.

"Steve," I said to my husband, "if we're going to keep Stripey, I think we'd better have her fixed."

"I don't think we need to have her fixed," he said with a sheepish look, "because she's going to have kittens."

Sure enough, a few weeks later, Stripey became a mother. Again, I told my husband, "Isn't it time to take Stripey to the vet?"

Time after time I got the same reply, "I'll take her next week."

In the spring, Stripey was due to have kittens again. One Saturday morning, she disappeared. We searched for her all weekend, but couldn't find her. We were so sad. On Monday morning, Steve called me from work.

"Guess who I found?"

"Who?"

"Stripey! I found her at work under a co-worker's truck. She must have gotten into the bed of my truck last week. I called her and she came right to me. I think she's really nervous so I'm going to bring her right home."

Great, I thought. We had all missed Stripey so much.

Steve walked in the house smiling and holding the cat.

"Stripey, you're home!" I cried.

I opened a can of her favorite food and she devoured it.

31

When we set her in the yard she looked confused.

"Oh, she's just had a rough weekend. She's really anxious about being home," I explained her nervousness away.

"She really lost weight," said Steve. I don't remember her ever being so lean."

"Poor thing," I said. "It's the lack of nutrition.

We stood watching her walk away and Steve said, "I don't remember that spot on her side."

He examined the cat more closely and upon realizing it was a male, he proudly exclaimed, "Honey, I fixed the cat!"

MAMA'S KNEES
By Esther Pérez Martín
Dedicated to my mother, Elvira Garcia Vargas

"Are you sure you want to take all three kids to Safeway?"

"It's no trouble, Esther. Really." My husband was so convincing, it made me smile. He wanted to make up for snapping at me while we made the grocery list.

"All right. But keep an eye on them. They're not the angels you think they are."

" I know how to handle children. I'll just put all three of them in the cart and let them help. They just need to feel important."

"Okay, Daniel. It will give me a chance to clean out the refrigerator."

I didn't expect them back so soon. Car doors slammed, children whined, and Daniel's angry voice boomed.

I opened the door. "Back so soon? Where's the groceries?"

"That is the last time I take these diablitos (little devils) shopping!"

All three children hugged my knees. "I thought you were letting them help," I said.

"Every time I wasn't looking they put in everything within reach. We filled the cart to the top in no time. Then I decided to buy just one more thing. We were on the cookie aisle and I only looked away for a moment, Esther, I swear. These three reached over to grab the goodies and turned the cart over. Everything fell. The kids, the vegetables, the fruit, everything. There were broken eggshells and spilled juice all over. I got so embarrassed, I picked up the kids and the cart and left the mess. We can't go back there."

"You want me to do the shopping?" I asked.

"What? Are you crazy? You're not leaving me here with **them**. I'll go alone this time."

As the door slammed, and the kids continued to hug my knees and sniffle, I had to smile. It brought back a fond memory.

My brother Raul and I were easily entertained when we were small. One day we wanted to jump rope, but didn't have one. So we used a hoe instead. I swung and Raul jumped.

"Twenty-two, twenty-three…," my brother counted.

"Okay, Rulo," I said. "I'm getting tired and dizzy swinging this hoe."

"Wait till I miss. Thirty-five, thirty-six…"

"Really, Rulo. Let me have a turn."

"Not yet. Forty-one, forty-two…"

The thought came to me before it was even a thought. It was more like instinct. I raised the hoe higher than his feet and hit him in the ankles. He stopped jumping and glared at me, tears flowing.

I dropped the hoe and ran.

"You're gonna get it Esther!"

I ran in the house and found myself hugging Mama's knees, hiding my face in her apron. There was nothing like the safety of Mama's knees.

Esther Pérez Martín is a 20-year veteran of the Fresno Police Department. She and her husband of 34 years have three wonderful children. Esther's passion is writing poetry. She is published in five books: Treasured Poems of America, 1998, Poetry's Elite, 2000, Awakening to Sunshine, National Library / A Whispering Silence, and A Celebration of Poets. She has also done readings at women's conferences and workshops. In all her writings, the main theme is family.

THE LITTLE WHITE TERRIER
By Richard G. Flores, Sr.
Dedicated to Isabelle, my wife of 54 years
Also to my kids, Richard, Carlos, and Rita, my grandchildren and great-grandkids (who know more about life than I did at their age).

When I was five years old my mother enrolled me in Lincoln Elementary School, six blocks from home. I was given the responsibility of caring for my older sister.

"Hold your sister's hand, Dickie, and don't let anything happen to her." It made me feel like a big boy.

Nearby was a mortuary, one block west of "G" Street on San Benito. It was scary walking through there because that's where they kept dead people. But it wasn't the corpses that scared me.

Inside, the owners had a little white dog. He didn't like me and I was afraid of him. I once heard a kid say it was a terrier. I imagined he was a breed that made kids feel terror. My legs wobbled each time I saw him.

Every day, whether we were on our way to or from school, he lay in wait. It seemed like he knew the exact time we'd be passing. I believed he sensed my fear and always came out barking and snarling.

One day he chased us and my sister tripped, almost hurting herself. "We should tell Mom," she said.

"No. Mom might yell at those people. What if they get mad and stick us in a casket? Besides, Mom will think I'm a fraidy-cat."

It never occurred to me to take a different route. Instead, I endured the fear and suffered in silence. Responsibility was not easy.

*Richard G. Flores, Sr. retired from the U.S. Postal Service after 38 years of service. He was born in Fresno, "the heart of California", and attended Lincoln and Columbia elementary schools, Edison High School, Fresno City College, Fresno State, and U.C. Berkeley during his tenure in the Marine Corps. He recently retired from a second career and is working on stories about his early life in Fresno for the benefit of his great-grandchildren.

SPAGHETTI SAUCE AND BEEF JERKY
By Nancy C. Ray
Dedicated to Mickey and Grandma Celeste

Grandma's house always smelled of spaghetti sauce. She cooked it twice a week, every week. Meatballs and lamb gave it a unique but familiar aroma. It teased my taste buds and made my stomach growl.

"Mickey, come to Grandma." That was the first thing she always said when we arrived. After-all, Mickey was like a grandchild. "Now go find Grandpa."

Mickey Schnauzer loved those visits. My husband knew I'd grown up being a dog lover. When we bought our first house he surprised me with a Mini-Schnauzer for Christmas. I gave her full run of the house and took her everywhere; jogging, shopping, on vacations to New Mexico, Oklahoma and Lake Tahoe. I even took her to Disneyland to visit her namesake.

Mickey won everybody's heart. Every visit to Grandma's was a pleasurable experience. Everyone wanted to play with her and give her treats. I bought only the best for her, including beef jerky treats that looked like the real thing. I bought them at a select pet store. As usual, I brought along a plastic baggy full of them and placed them on the kitchen counter till Mickey's feeding time.

My sisters arrived, bearing specialty dishes. We placed them all on the counter and went into the family room to watch TV while the spaghetti sauce simmered.

"What do you think Bill will bring?" I asked with sarcasm.

"The same thing he always brings," said Deborah, "his appetite."

"And his opinionated mouth," quipped Dorothy.

My brother had never been one to bring anything to family dinners. "He is such a tightwad," I said. "Poor guy'll never change."

Sure enough, Bill arrived empty-handed. We couldn't see him from where we sat, but my sisters and I could hear him making critical remarks about the dishes we'd brought.

"Shut up Bill," we took turns saying.

Then suddenly his voice got louder. "Yuck! Who brought **these**? They're terrible!

We ran into the kitchen and saw Bill spitting bits of Mickey's doggy beef jerky into the trash. We laughed so hard it hurt.

To top it off, Mickey stood and barked at Bill like she was lecturing him for wasting her food.

"Oh, what payback," said Deborah, tears rolling down her cheeks.

"Everybody knows that's Mickey's food," said Dorothy, holding her sides.

Ten years have passed since the doggy treat incident. It has become one of our favorite memories. Mickey passed away in my arms from a heart attack a year ago. It comforts my sister and me to think she is keeping Grandma company in heaven.

PREGNANCY AND HUNGER

By Nancy C. Ray
Dedicated to Missy Michelle(y) and Mom

My daughter, Nicolette and I were a mile from the restaurant when I pulled off the freeway. Something didn't feel right.

"Mom, what's wrong? You don't look right."

I didn't want to frighten her with my premonition. "Nothing, honey. I guess I'm just excited that my twin sister is going to have a baby."

"Why didn't we ride together with Grandma Celeste and aunt Dorothy?"

"Oh, you don't want to be in the same car with a pregnant woman, do you? Look, there's the restaurant."

My mind raced. I couldn't explain my apprehension. I felt like something violent was going to happen. My mom and sister were waiting for us. I decided to keep my thoughts to myself.

As we entered the restaurant I noticed two women, and two men sitting on the porch and assessed them carefully. They looked out of place. *Were they waiting for someone?*

The waitress sat us at a table in the middle of the room, Mom and Dorothy on one side, Nicolette and I on the other. The place was full to capacity. I scoped out the layout, checking where the kitchen, hallways, and all the exits were located.

"Nancy, is something wrong?" asked Mom.

"I don't like this place. I can't believe you come here. It's not my kind of restaurant."

"It's not a bad place," said Mom, picking up her menu.

Dorothy could read me better than anyone. She patted my hand. "Don't worry. The people are nice and the food is real good."

The first course arrived, soup of the day. It was delicious. Then the salad. I began to relax. Then the main course, a Calamari steak in all its glory. That is when I decided my premonition had been wrong.

Each of us was cutting into our Calamari when a sound like firecrackers from outside broke the silence. Glass and drywall were being sprayed all over our table. One of the men I had seen on the front porch emptied his guns, firing eight to ten shots. Everyone dove to the floor.

"Crawl to the kitchen!" ordered the waitress.

All of us did. Except one.

Crowded in the kitchen, we waited for police to arrive, too frightened to move. After several minutes, the waitress stepped out, then came back into the kitchen shaking her head.

"I can't believe there is still a woman in there eating. And she wants more salad."

I braved a peak into the seating area, and there was Dorothy, sitting at the table eating.

"Are you nuts?" I called. "There could be glass fragments and drywall in your food."

"But I'm hungry! I'm really hungry," said Dorothy.

Michelle was born July, 2000.

WILL I SEE MY FATHER?

By Eluid M. Romero

Dedicated to my wife, Sylvia and my daughters, Syvie and Andrea

"You have a 98% chance of surviving this operation." The surgeon's voice echoed inside my head. *This can't be happening.* With those odds, two out of every hundred persons getting the same surgery would actually die! *What if I'm in the unfortunate two percent?*

The surgeon must have noticed my concern. He quickly chimed in, "These are really pretty good odds. If we were having this conversation just fifteen years ago, I would be telling you the odds were fifty-fifty."

My mind raced as I sat with my wife in the doctor's office. Diplomas and various academic certificates decorated the walls. He proceeded to describe the procedure for a heart bypass operation much as a mechanic might explain to a novice the procedure for tuning up an engine.

"We will have to cut the sternum, or breastbone, of course, to give us access to your heart. You will be on a ventilator that will handle the breathing for you. Then we will have to divert your blood to a heart lung machine that will circulate your blood, while we stop your heart in order to do the necessary repairs."

The rest of the explanation floated over my head and into oblivion. The realization came over me that this was serious. This was life or death! This man was telling me that in a week my body would be opened and my heart stopped for repairs. *Would it start up again? What if they waited too long?* I don't even remember the ride home.

For the next several days, many thoughts circulated through my brain. *How could this be? Why me?* I had been relatively healthy all my life. I had worked twenty-seven years and never missed work for illness other than colds or flu. How could my heart have so many areas blocked? I could name several people with diets much worse than mine. What should I do for the next few days? After all, these may be my last!

Genetics, the surgeon explained, was a huge risk factor. Just five months earlier, my father had suffered a heart attack and passed away. At least my blockages were discovered early. This gave me greater odds for survival and making a full recovery. Did I feel lucky? No!

Do I have enough insurance? What if I don't survive? Should I prepare an obituary? What picture will they use in the newspaper? I didn't have any recent pictures I liked. Maybe I could go on a crash diet and then snap a last minute Polaroid?

I only had a week and I didn't know if I was ready for the challenge of my life. Had I done everything I wanted in my fifty three years? Maybe a trip would be good, but where would I go? Maybe a few drinks would make me feel better? But then again, I wouldn't want to go into surgery with a hangover!

Was I spiritually ready? Of course I had to go to confession. There could be no holding back or cheating on this one. I had to remember everything I had done in my life, as this could be the only chance I would have to ask forgiveness. Crazy thoughts popped into my head. That party in college when my two male friends passed out and I took off all their clothes and put them in the same bed together. They always wondered how they got there, and I never told them. How about the time I called my mother-in-law and pretended to be her doctor. She had proceeded to tell me several embarrassing and personal health problems, until I could no longer keep from laughing. The time in college when I sneaked into the priest's side of the church confessional and my friends encouraged some mutual friends to come in and confess. At least I never disclosed the sins they told me. Did I have to confess all that? And there was much more.

The days flew by. Time had suddenly accelerated and there was nothing I could do to slow it down. As the date of my surgery approached, I begin to question whether I could go through with it. Was it fear that I wouldn't survive? Was it fear that I would survive but suffer extreme pain? Was it a realization that even if I survived, my life would be changed forever? It was all the above.

41

When the day arrived, the alarm woke me from a restless sleep. I went through the motions of getting ready, trying not to think of what may lie ahead. We drove to the hospital, and they had a room ready for me. Then suddenly, a whole series of events began unfolding. I had barely changed to a gown and begun to relax in bed, when a nurse started shaving my chest and arms and legs. "We might need to get an artery from your arm or leg for the bypass," she explained.

An IV was started on my neck. Blood was withdrawn for last minute tests. Through all of this I was resigned to go in and get it over with. But just as all the preparation was completed, came the news that my eleven a.m. surgery would be delayed because the surgeon's first bypass of the day was taking longer than anticipated. An hour, then two, then three went by. Even though my wife and daughters were holding my hand, I was beginning to get scared. Anxiety started to take over my body, and I had the urge to unplug all the needles, get my clothes back on, and get as far away from there as possible.

Just as I reached the breaking point, an interesting thought entered my mind. *What if I don't survive? Will I see my father?* Since he had lived far away from me the last years of his life, I had not gotten to see him as often as I wished. There were several things I wished I would have said to him before he passed away. Was it possible that this very day, in just a matter of minutes, I would see and talk to him? The thought overwhelmed me, and gave me a calmness I can't describe.

Eventually, they came and rolled me to the surgery room, started injecting solutions into the IV in my neck, and all I remember is trying to think of what to say to Dad. My anxiety was gone as I lost consciousness. My only thought: *Will I see my father?*

*Eluid Romero has been married to his wife, Sylvia for twenty-seven years. They have two daughters, Syvie and Andrea. He is a graduate of Santa Clara University and has a law degree from McGeorge School of Law in Sacramento. He is Supervision Attorney with the Sacramento County Public Defender where he's been employed for the past twenty-eight years. He is in charge of various sections of the office, including Major Crimes and Capital cases, and the Drug Courts. He also supervises and trains attorneys in the felony and misdemeanor sections.

Where's the Nut?
By Heidi Thompson
Dedicated to my son, Martin

I had heard of a way to explain death to young children. When my 97-year-old great grandmother Adda passed away I was discussing the explanation with my mother. She took my four-year-old son for a walk and when the subject came up, she gave it a try.

"Grandma, who will Adda see in heaven?" asked Martin.

"Well, let's see, who do we know in heaven? Papa, your dogs Roy and Winnie, your goldfish, is there anyone else?"

"I don't think so," after a long pause, "How does she eat now?"

"Well, Martin she doesn't need to eat. She's different now."

"What do you mean she's different?"

"Have you ever seen a nut before, like a peanut or a walnut?"

"Yeah."

"You know how there's a shell you have to break off before you get to the inside part that you eat?"

"Yeah."

"Well, imagine Adda is like a nut. The only thing that's left of her on earth is the shell. The inside part, the part that is most important, is gone. When she died, the shell of her body was left on earth but the inside of her, her soul, left earth and went to heaven."

"Oh."

He seemed satisfied with the explanation so they continued their walk and talked about the birds they saw, the concrete truck that was building a pool, and the bugs that were crawling on the sidewalk.

When they got back I asked how their walk had been.

"It was great. Martin and I had a really good talk," my mom said.

I turned my attention to Martin, "What did you talk about?"

43

"We talked about dead things," he said.

"You did? What did you learn about them?" I asked.

He thought for a moment, and then said, "Grandma says when people die, they look like nuts."

At the memorial Martin was sitting next to his dad. He was quiet, as he seemed to be listening to the speakers and the songs. His eyes were fixed on the closed casket in front of the church. Near the end of the service he leaned over to my husband and asked, "Dad, is the nut in the box?"

*Heidi Thompson is a full-time mom and teaches second grade. Though she enjoys her job, she hopes to make writing a career one day. Her wish is that her stories will bring smiles to her children and their children after them. Until then, she will continue to love and educate youngsters at home and at school every day.

THE WALNUT SHELL
By Margretta Schleich
Dedicated to Martha Linkugel

In the early 1950's, Martha taught Sunday School at Trinity Lutheran Church in Baldwin park, California. Her classes were full of four and five year-olds. They were an active group requiring a variety of songs and stories. What their voices lacked in tone and clarity, was made up for in fervor.

One year, her class included four kids who were all first cousins and shared the same grandparents. The kids all showed up for class the Sunday after their grandfather died. As they walked in, Martha knew something was wrong. The kids were fidgety and sad-looking. She tried to get them talking, but their heads drooped and they stared at the floor.

Finally, one of the boys blurted out, "Our parents lied to us."

The others nodded in agreement. They seemed so hurt and confused that Martha stopped the class to talk to them. When asked what happened, they all told her that their parents' lied when they said Grandpa went to heaven. They knew he didn't. They had been taken to a place and Grandpa was in this big beautiful bed. He wasn't in heaven. He was in the wood bed. Martha uttered a silent prayer asking what to say. Suddenly the words came to her and she asked if they knew what a walnut looks like. They nodded.

"Have you all cracked walnuts? If you are very careful, the walnut can be separated into two perfect halves. You can take the shell apart and take out the part you eat. Then if you put the shell back together, it will look just like it did before."

The kids nodded in agreement. They all had cracked and shelled walnuts. The class remained silent.

"Now, if you put a whole walnut in the ground, the part you eat will grow into a tree. That is the life of the nut. The shell holds this life and protects it. God took the life out of your Grandfather and what was left was his body or shell. We call the life part a soul. It is the part of you that makes you, you. This is what God takes to heaven. He leaves the shell behind for us.

"Then we take the shell and have a funeral. We put the body in a fancy bed. The bed is closed up and taken to a place called a cemetery. Then we put the bed into the ground. This is what happened to your Grandpa, but his life went to heaven."

The children's faces brightened. They understood.

"This is our memory of a time when Mom, Martha Linkugel Maurer, helped others find their way. We have used it to help children and adults understand some things about death and faith."

*Margretta Schleich, Martha's daughter, is a Licensed Clinical Social Worker, who has had words given to her in answer to prayers too. She is currently writing a cookbook based on fifty years of recipe collecting. GRANNIE GRETTA'S SALADS, SOUPS, STEWS, AND COVERED DISHES will be released in 2004 by Copy Grounds (www.copy grounds.com).

THE FUNERAL
By Lupe Sánchez Garcia
Dedicated to my sisters, brother, and all our cousins

Vera walked out of the house clutching a small glass fishbowl to her chest. Tears rolled down her cheeks.

"What's wrong, Vera? What happened?"

"It's Goldie. He's dead."

It was 1943. There was a war. We lived in a place called Harbor Gate, which does not exist anymore. It was government housing, provided for the people that worked in the shipyards. The houses bordered a large common green lawn where we could play. Beyond was the Pacific Ocean.

There were fifteen of us, all first cousins (five my dad's, five Tío Juan's, and five Tío Gilberto's). We only went to school half days. Grandma Bernardina and Grandpa Vicente kinda watched over us, while our parents worked. It was up to us to watch out for each other and occupy the rest of the day.

Cousin Vera, six, was heart broken over her goldfish and cried and cried. The rest of us, ranging in age from three to nine, tried to console her. Gilbert, Esther and I finally decided to have a funeral for her goldfish. Not just any funeral. We sat around and made plans.

"We can do just like in the movies. We'll need everyone to help," I said.

Esther added, "Yes, that will take Vera's mind off the tragedy."

"What'll I do?" asked Gilberto.

"Well, you need to be the priest 'cause you're the oldest boy. And Esther, you direct the choir. We can't do it right without singin' like they do in church. And, I will be the boss."

We found a matchbox. We put a small piece of cloth inside, laid Goldie on top, and slid the box closed. All the cousins gathered and were sent home to dress for the service. Decked out in our best clothes, we marched out to the field. We picked a place where Goldie could see the Pacific Ocean. We dug a hole and placed the box next to it.

Each of us had a role to play. We had "Criers" who stood with Vera and cried on command. We had a choir who sang on cue. Gilbert, "Tito", said the "Our Fathers" and "Hail Marys."

After each somber "Hail Mary I would say "Cry" and the criers would wail. My sister, Tina, dabbed at her eyes with her hankie. Virgie grabbed Vera's shoulders and sobbed. When I said, "Stop," they stopped.

Following the "Our Fathers," I nodded and the choir started singing. Jennie, Mary, Ellen, Rita, and Esther sang and hugged each other at the proper times. We sang "Rock of Ages," a hymn we learned in school.

The youngest cousins, Manuel, Louie, and Carmen stared at the small box on the ground. We each picked up some dirt and put it on the box. Gilbert tied two sticks together and we placed the cross over the burial site. Vera was pleased.

I don't think any fish ever had such an elaborate, well-planned funeral or was laid to rest with more pomp and fanfare than Vera's Goldie.

Now we are old men and women in our 60's and 70's. When we get together, we still talk about the funeral.

*Lupe Garcia lived in Glendale, Arizona until her family moved to California to work in the war effort. After the war, the family worked as migrant farm laborers. They moved to Madera, California when she was twelve. In 1952, she was the first Hispanic to speak at a high school graduation. She married and had three children, six grandchildren, and three great-grandchildren. She worked for Madera County from High School graduation until her retirement. After a few years off, she retuned to the Human Services Office as a translator, and is paid to talk (after all those years of her cousins trying to shut her up).

TELL HIM I'M NOT HERE
By Tom Wilkes
Dedicated to John and Janet Flinn

Janet and Johnny met in grammar school and experienced puppy love. They were like glue, always together, walking to and from school, holding hands, and sharing secrets. It was an awkward age for both of them and it seemed as if they were made for each other. I couldn't decide which of them was clumsiest. Like any big brother, I teased Janet every chance I got.

As they grew older, Janet began to blossom and receive attention from other boys. Requests for dates and invitations to parties boosted her ego, but didn't sit well with Johnny. After all, she was his girl. His self-confidence must have dwindled because he started trying hard to impress her, smothering her with attention.

Johnny immediately applied for a learners permit, and at age sixteen, got his driver's license. Sometimes he came over without his dad knowing, and without telling Janet.

One night Johnny came over unexpectedly. The porch light shone on his tall, thin frame. He was dressed like he was ready for a date.

"Janet, it's for you," I said, after the initial knock.

"Don't open the door," she whispered.

"But it's Johnny. Didn't you hear the car?"

"Tell him I'm not here."

"I'm not getting in the middle of this," I said, sitting back down on the easy chair.

Dad was asleep on the couch, peaceful as a pup. He was a large man, pleasant and slow to anger. But he hated to have his sleep disturbed.

Janet shook him. I cringed.

"Wha..?"

"Dad, Johnny's at the door."

"Well, let him in, for Pete's sakes!"

"No," said Janet, "tell him I'm not here."

Dad got up, eyes red, hair disheveled. He tried to button his pajama top and the stubble on his chin made a scratching sound.

Johnny knocked louder.

Dad popped the door open and Johnny's eyes widened.

"Is Janet here?"

"She says she's not," said Dad.

Johnny just stood there, mouth open. I thought he was going to cry.

"Didn't you hear? She says she's not home!" Dad slammed the door and turned off the porch light, then lay back on the couch.

"Dad!" Janet's eyebrows arched and her mouth made a circle like she was holding an upright lifesaver. She turned and stomped into her room.

Eventually, the lovebirds got married. Once in a while Johnny teases Dad by asking if Janet is home. And incidentally, this is the only story I can tell about Janet without getting killed.

*Tom Wilkes is a retired Postal Employee from Fresno, California. So is his sister, Janet. She retired from Clovis Post Office. Tom claims he became well-suited to work for the Postal Service during his youth, when he delivered the Fresno Bee newspaper on his bicycle. At the time, the newspaper was a dollar and a half per month. "And even then, I often got stiffed for the money," he claims. He was often chased by dogs and got bit on both legs at one time or another. His worst memory was one particular house where the owners had two dogs. The brown one attacked from the left and the white one from the right. One day they both got a bite out of him.

CALIFORNIA DREAMING
By Berta Guerra
Dedicated to my sister, Norma

We were ten brothers and sisters when we lived in Arizona. Robert was the oldest, then John, Mary, Joe, Jess, Emma, Lucy, Norma, me, and Carmen. Dad worked in the copper mines and Mom was a housewife. The money was good, and we lacked for nothing.

My brother Joe had a little candy store in our basement, and used a bucket of urine, propped on top of the door to discourage robbers (mainly my other brothers and sisters). I was too young to care about anything.

Reality hit hard when my brother John left to join the army and my mom took the younger kids to California to force Dad to leave the mines. She was afraid he'd get the dreaded Black Lung Disease. We were all excited, except my sister Mary, who left behind tons of boyfriends.

We arrived in Parlier in a settlement appropriately named, The Jungle. My tía Lupe lived there and let us put a large canvas tent on her property. My cousin Armando loved to eat tortillas with Mayonnaise. He'd give me some and we'd try to feed it to my tío José's cow. I'd hold it in my outstretched hand and tell the cow, "toma (take)". Eventually, everyone called the cow Toma.

Grapes were plentiful and there were wild berries in the forest. We'd put holes near the tops of empty coffee cans and run a wire through them to make small buckets to pick fruit. There was an abundance of peach boxes to use as tables and chairs. Cousin Armando and I would ride the butane tank and shoot make-believe cowboys. For snacks, we'd enjoy warm, delicious milk and grapes wrapped in homemade tortillas. If we dropped a grape, we'd look for it in the rocks till we found it. Life was good. In time we moved to other small towns, and eventually settled in

Selma.

Norma and I are exactly two years apart. I was told she ran around in circles when Mom brought me home from the hospital. I don't know if she was jealous or glad to have someone she could beat up on. But she and I grew up close. She's always been my defender, confidant and best friend. We still argue and fight like sisters, but always make up with "I love you."

I was a second grader at Washington Elementary when we moved to Selma, and Norma was in fourth. Our dresses were homemade with 'olanes', rows and rows of material going round and round our bodies, secured with a bow in the back. One day a tough kid picked a fight with me, and as usual, I ran and hid behind Norma. She was not one to back down from anyone. She put her hands on her hips and bad-mouthed the kid till he got red. He responded by reaching behind her and pulling on the bow. He pulled so hard that she started going round and round till she was left standing in her slip. She yelled one more cuss word at the kid, grabbed my hand and walked away with me in tow. I'll never forget how she fought that fight for me, along with many others.

*Berta Guerra is a retired Postal employee, now working in education. She has two children and two granddaughters. She and her family reside in Fresno, California.

SNAKE IN THE GRASS
By Janet Stutzman
Dedicated to my daughter, Hannah

I pushed the key into the lock, balancing a grocery bag on my hip. Before I could turn it, Hannah flung the door wide.

"Mom! You gotta help me catch the snake!"

"What snake?" I asked, setting the groceries on the table.

She ran to the family room, dropped to her knees and peered under the sofa.

"It's in the house?" I asked.

"Yeah. But I don't know where."

"How did it get in the house?"

"I was bringing it in to show Dad and it jumped out of the bowl. And Dad wouldn't let me catch it until he took his pants off."

Exasperated, Hannah crawled around the room peering under each piece of furniture.

"What?" I asked, "Why would he want his pants off before you caught the snake?"

Hannah rose to her knees and faced me. "Well, he was trying to get his feet out," she explained. "And by the time he did, the snake was gone."

"You mean the snake was *in* his pants?" I asked.
Hannah nodded.

"How in the heck…"

"I found a snake in the back yard. I put it in a bowl," Hannah explained, as if to an imbecile. "I took it in the house to show Dad, and it jumped out of the bowl. Dad was taking his pants off to put on his swim trunks and the snake landed right in his pants."

"Now," she continued, "We have to find it. It's so small it could really get lost in here."

"What kind of snake are we looking for?"

"It's just a little garter snake. I don't know why Dad got so excited."

"I can't imagine," I said, smiling.

Steve had no idea what he was getting into when he vowed, "For better or for worse."

I got down on the floor to help search. "Well, where did it go?"

"After Dad got his pants off, it slithered under the recliner."

Hannah and I searched the room and found the six-inch visitor behind a video case. It crawled into my hand, serpentine scales gleaming like tiny jewels.

No wonder she wanted to show it to her dad!

Together, we took it into the front yard and released it on the lawn. Within seconds, perfectly camouflaged, it disappeared before our eyes.

"That's *awesome*!" Hannah breathed.

"Yeah, it sure is," I said.

Steve was nowhere to be found.

THE HUGE HUGO FAMILY
By Sandy Chabot
Dedicated to Mom and Dad

My parents, John and Carol raised a large family. By the time Mom was twenty-nine, she had eight kids. First there was Debbie, then Chuck, me, Diane, Gail, John Jr., Rick, and Vonda. We lived in a large city in California before moving to the suburbs of Minneapolis and St. Paul. Eventually, we ended up on a small hobby farm in Hugo, Minnesota.

Our family was poor and all the children had to help with chores and housework when my parents were at work. We had little time for after school activities. Times were tough but it made us a closer family. We often sit around and tell stories of our childhood.

When I was thirteen, every day Mom would write a list of jobs for each of us while she and Dad worked the evening shift. Because ours was a small hobby farm, we didn't have all the fancy farm equipment and many of the chores were done by hand. Every so often I had to milk our cow, Bessie. I was a tiny child with small hands so this activity was difficult for me. I also hated the smell of cow poop and didn't like getting dirty. When it was my turn to milk Bessie, I would tie a scarf around my mouth and nose. I would tie Bessie's dirty tail to the fence so she couldn't hit me with it. My mom expected us to get a full pail of milk, but I was too lazy and would only fill it half way. To trick Mom, I would add water to make it look full. We never told her until I was older. She became very upset anyway, because we could have ruined the cow.

My younger sister, Diane was eight years old when we owned several ponies. One of them, Beauty, liked to bite people. One day Diane was wearing a shirt with an apple design. We were standing next to the fence petting the ponies when Beauty bit a hole right through the front of Diane's shirt. She must have thought the apple was real. Diane started to cry. The rest of us laughed.

Every weekend, Mom made us spend several hours in the garden pulling weeds. We hated it but had no choice. We would get bored and tell Mom we had to go to the bathroom, but instead we'd sit in the house and sneak ice cream and other treats while watching everyone else outside working. If we took too much time, Mom would come looking for us and yell.

One day my sisters Diane and Gail and I were playing a game called footsie. It is a plastic cup on a string that you put on your ankle and circle around and jump over. We were supposed to be doing yard work and my dad came in the house looking for us. The three of us were scared at being yelled at so we hid in a closet. We were all giggling so loud my dad heard us. He pulled us out of the dark closet, one at a time, hit us and told us to get outside. I was the last one in the closet and had the footsie on my ankle which made it hard to get up and walk. My dad kept kicking me and yelling at me to get outside. I was crying hard but later we all laughed about it. Dad never hit hard enough to hurt us.

*Sandy Chabot is Customer Relations Coordinator for the St. Paul Postmaster. She has a degree in Marketing/Business. She started her UPSP career in 1981 and has held several administrative positions. She enjoys travel, cooking, reading, motorcycling, and riding her snowmobile. Her husband, Dale, is a building maintenance engineer with the USPS. They have two grown children, Brian, 25 and Jennifer, 21.

THE SHORTEST ROUTE
By Dorothy Plummer
Dedicated to the Romero family

"Mama, why aren't they here yet?" Those were the anxious words of our youngest daughter, Diana. Not quite five years old, we called her our little 'Worry-wart'.

"Be patient," I told her, "it's a long way." Our other three children were just as anxious, but managed to keep quiet about it.

It was the summer vacation-from-school time, and we were awaiting the arrival of my youngest aunt, her husband and five of their seven children. I had been raised by her parents, my grandparents, on a small farm in New Mexico. Although she was nine years my senior, we grew up just like sisters. Her children, ranging in age from seven to twenty-five, were very precious to me. They now lived in California, except for the two oldest girls, who were married.

We had moved from New Mexico, where both our families had been close and dear to each other, to a small farm in Idaho. Our four children were joyously awaiting the fun that would ensue from the visit of their five cousins, Aunt Edilia, and Uncle Manuel. Louie, their oldest son, owned a 1966 Thunderbird, and would be the driver.

I was becoming concerned when they did not arrive long after we had expected them. They had called from Rogerson, twenty miles past the Nevada border into Idaho and less than a hundred miles away.

Finally, Diana, jumping up and down, shouted, "They're here!"

Good. It was about time. All the food I carefully prepared would need to be re-warmed. I had cooked a big pot of pinto beans and another of red chile, foods we had all enjoyed in New Mexico. These kept well, and would be easy to reheat without losing flavor. I had also baked a big batch of homemade bread the day before. But the food getting cold had been the least of our worries. We feared, after waiting so long, that there may have been an accident.

Thank the Lord they all seemed fine as the car came to a stop and they stepped out. They looked tired, dusty, and a little dazed as they clambered out of their small car, all seven of them.

"Now the fun can begin," said our nine year-old son, David, who usually considered himself grown-up and serious. It was a joy to see how happy both families were to be together once more.

After the excitement and joyous greetings and exclamations of "My goodness, how much you have grown," from the adults about all the children, we settled down for a meal.

Having eaten, the eight youngest children went outdoors to unwind and see our farm animals. Louie, a 'young adult', who looked tired from driving, joined the rest of the grownups as we sat down to our exchange of news and remember-when session. I was then finally able to ask my Aunt Edilia why it had taken them so long to arrive.

"Because your roads are terrible," she said, "and you moved so far away." She was obviously agitated. After a short pause for breath, she continued, "I don't see why you came to such a distant place with such horrible roads. How in the world do you ever go anywhere to do your shopping or anything?"

This really puzzled us, since we were only twenty miles, over excellent paved roads, from a large town. Aside from a grocery store, our tiny town of Oakley had a post office, theatre, gas station, and hardware store. Though it was only a two-street community serving the surrounding farms, it was only two miles from us. And those two miles were also paved.

"What do you mean by poor roads," I asked. "It's not far, and the road to Rogerson is only a two-lane highway, but is in excellent condition."

"You must certainly not be talking about the same road we took," snorted my uncle Manuel. "The road we came on started out as gravel, then quickly turned to dirt, and went up and down and around trees and hills and what-not." He went on to describe how they had precariously skirted steep cliffs and had trouble going over the bumps and ruts in places. "Boy, I dread going back over that mess again on the way home." He shook his head and whistled. "We damaged the bumper," he added.

"What were you doing on such a road?" This came from me.

My husband, Gene was beginning to grin. "How in the world did you get on *that* road?" He apparently knew the road being described. "From Rogerson you stay on the highway to Twin Falls. From there, the same good highway goes to Burley, and from there to here it's only twenty-two miles, all on good roads.

"We saw a man on horseback just outside of Rogerson," said my uncle. "He was near the entrance to a road that had a sign that said OAKLEY. We asked him if that was the shortest route and he said yes."

Sputtering with laughter, Gene was finally able to get out the words which cleared the mystery. "That may be the shortest distance, but it certainly isn't the quickest route. That was the forest service road up from Rogerson on up to Magic Mountain, the ski area. It's a little over fifty miles of gravel and dirt over mountains and valleys. You can quit worrying yourself about going back on poor roads. There's a good two-lane paved highway back."

Uncle Manuel laughed, enjoying the joke played on them. He could see the humor of the man sending Californians through the shortest distance over that road in a tiny car packed with seven people over hot, dusty and not-so-safe roads. But all my Aunt Edilia was able to say upon hearing Gene's words was, "Thank God."

Considering the lovely ensuing visit, we hope it was well worth the discomfort of that memorable trip for our loved ones. We were so very grateful to them for it.

*Dorothy Plummer is a retired school teacher and farmer's wife. She lives in Deming, New Mexico with her husband of forty-five years.

WHEN THONGS WERE SHOES
By Ben Romero
Dedicated to my three daughters

She needed summer shoes, something comfortable, practical and inexpensive.

My wife, Evelyn walked in the front door, a pair of yellow thongs in her hand. "Look I what I have for you." It made sense. They were easy to slip on and off, yet sturdy enough for a nine-year-old. "They'll be perfect for our trip to the beach."

"I wanted Jellies," said Victoria, obviously disappointed.

"What's *that*?" I asked.

"They're those new plastic shoes girls are wearing," said Evelyn. "They come in bright colors and have holes all over."

"Are they expensive?"

"Nah," said Evelyn shaking her head, "about five bucks."

Victoria's eyes pleaded.

"Buy her a pair tomorrow," I said.

Victoria smiled, her teeth gleaming in contrast to suntanned skin.

Evelyn shook her head. She often said I let the kids wrap me around their little finger, but her body language told me she'd be glad to go shopping again.

"Look Dad, they're purple!" She walked around the house like Cinderella showing off glass slippers.

"They look flimsy to me," said my son, Andy, trying to step on her feet.

"Leave your sister alone," I cautioned. "You're older and bigger than her, but she's got a temper."

"We're here!" Andy and Victoria raced to the water, Andy in sandals, Victoria wearing Jellies. My wife and I walked slowly. I held my son Gabriel's hand and Evelyn carried Rebecca.

"Hold on!" yelled Evelyn. Victoria was already ankle-deep in water and still running. A wave formed and she turned around, trying to avoid it. She got knocked down, Jellies floating in foamy, brown seawater.

"Are you all right?"

"My Jelly!" Each wave carried it farther.

Several years later we were planning a trip to the same beach. Andy and Victoria were grown, married, and out of the house. Gabriel and Rebecca were sophisticated teenagers, and my youngest daughter, Olivia was seven years old.

"We don't want to make the same mistake we made when we bought Victoria Jellies," I told Evelyn. "Why don't you buy Olivia a pair of thongs for the beach."

"I wouldn't wear one of those things in public," said Olivia, wrinkling her forehead Rebecca snickered.

"Why not?" I asked, more confused than ever.

"I'm not letting the world see my butt."

"What are you talking about?"

"Thongs are underwear," said Evelyn.

"Since when? I can't see how anybody could use them for underwear."

"No, you're not listening to me." She stood close and stared into my eyes like she needed to connect with my brain. "They sell intimate underwear called thongs."

I looked around. Rebecca and Gabriel were giggling.

"So what do you call the shoes now?"

"I don't know. Maybe they're called Zorries again, like in the old days."

I hate to think what I'd be referring to if I used the word Jellies.

WAYWARD JELLY
By Victoria Romero-Delsid
Dedicated to my daughters, Teniah and Mackyla

The day was hot. Seven of us were crammed into a car without air conditioning. I was nine, and wearing a brand new bathing suit and a pair of neon sunglasses. My getup was completed by a pair of purple Jellies, the latest craze in girls' footwear. They were a type of sandal made completely of transparent colored plastic and had a distinct smell that reminded me of a new baby doll.

We had been driving for what seemed an eternity. But none of that mattered now, because I could see the boardwalk. Santa Cruz had a year-round carnival and a beach. It was a magical place that made Daddy buy anything I asked for.

After an extensive search, we finally found a parking spot, and I was bursting with excitement, not so much for the beach, but because I knew when I got out of the car I would be a star. I just knew there would be movie cameras and people asking for my autograph. Reporters would ask how I managed to get a pair of Jellies.

I pushed my way out of the car, and letting my skin soak up the sun, I sucked in as much sea air as my lungs could handle. I looked around. No paparazzi. Oh, well. I knew it would still be a day I would never forget.

Getting the family of the car was an ordeal. Mom was crabby and trying to get my little brother and baby sister out. Dad was wrestling with the ice chest and lawn chairs. I was assisting with beach towels and diaper bags. My older brother, Andy, was fumbling with his radio and tapes.

Grandma stepped out of the car barking orders. She wore one of Mom's swimsuits. It was purple and white with a million little moons, and a little skirt. Her hair was in a bun, and she wore huge sunglasses. I was embarrassed and couldn't wait to get to the beach. I didn't want people to know I was with those hillbillies.

After all, I was a star.

"Everybody single-file!" That was a familiar line my mother yelled when she wanted us to walk together to avoid traffic. I took
Gabriel's hand and hurried along.

Finally, we were at the boardwalk. I took a moment to admire the sheer beauty of Santa Cruz beach. I could see heat waves rippling off the golden sand, and waves forming and crashing with a ribbon of foam.

I couldn't handle it any longer. I was about to explode like a volcano. Without forethought I dropped Gabriel's hand and broke into a sprint for the ocean.

I leapt from the last wooden step and my left foot hit glistening sand. Shock waves hit my brain like a lightning bolt and I realized Jelly shoes were not meant to be worn on hot sand.

"Victoria! Stop running!" I could hear my mother and grandmother yelling and knew I was in for the spanking of a lifetime if they caught me. But all I cared about was the smell of burning flesh. I could hear my feet sizzle. The faster I ran the worse it got. I hadn't realized how far it was.

I was still running when I hit the water. I swear I saw steam coming from my poor feet. What a relief. Then came my second miscalculation. I didn't realize how far into the water I had run. And I knew nothing about the power of waves.

The ocean roared like a lion. I looked up and caught a glimpse of wave as it crashed, knocking me over. My horror was not of being gobbled up by the wave, but rather the loss of my Jelly shoe.

I was in tears when I made it back to where the rest of the family set up a blanket. The bitter taste of salt lingered.

"I lost my Jelly," I managed to say, between sobs.

Everybody laughed.

"It isn't funny!" Those were the only shoes I brought and there was no way my mother would let me on the boardwalk without shoes. Dad eased my mind a little by telling me he'd swim far out and look for my shoe. Everyone else chimed in that they would aid in the effort.

Grandma set out to the right. "Victoria!" she yelled from a distance, "I saw your shoe but I was too slow to get it." How could she see it and let it get away? Old people frustrated me. *Well, at least there's hope.*

Eventually, the shoe was found. I wore my Jellies until they began falling apart. My father never hesitates to tell the Jelly story whenever he gets a chance. And yes, old people still frustrate me, but a little less with each passing year.

*Victoria Romero-Delsid is a Postal employee in Fresno, California. She and her husband, Justin, are raising two beautiful daughters. With little time for writing, she's content to read to her girls.

KIDNAPPED?

By George Vasquez
Dedicated to my sister, Antonia and my cousin, Grace

Before you jump to conclusions, let me make a few things clear: I do not have a hearing problem, nor am I a scare-dy cat.

Eight years ago, I was much the same person I am today. So it comes as no surprise that the day after my eleventh birthday, instead of playing with new toys and my new prized possession, Super Return of the Jedi for my Super Nintendo, I had a school project to work on. It should have been at least half-finished a month before, but hey, I'm sure something more important occupied my mind, preventing me from working on it.

At my parents insistence, or what I like to call nagging, I sat at the computer that Sunday afternoon doing my project. After several hours of semi-working, I saw the perfect opportunity for brief escape. My dad decided to leave the house to get a haircut, believing he could leave me alone to continue working diligently.

The moment I heard the sound of the garage door close, I proceeded to my forbidden indulgence. Flipping on the TV and loading my new game, fresh from its bubble wrap, I quickly entered a galaxy far, far away.

Fighting the forces of the dark side can put a lot of pressure on a fifth grader. As I sat there, in-between my two realities, an all too familiar sound echoed through my mind. It was the unmistakable sound of doors opening and closing, and it caused a definite tremor in the force. The problem was that I was home alone. I reasoned it may have been the radio, but turning off the volume and listening to the continued racket confirmed my fear. Someone was in the house.

I slithered into the kitchen, knowing I had to call my dad. He answered his cell phone, sounding annoyed.

"Hello?"

"Dad, I think there's someone in the house," I whispered.

"What! Are you sure?"

"I'm *pretty* sure I heard someone in your room."

"Well go and check."

"Uhhh." I was shocked my dad would ask me to search the house with the possibility someone was there, but he's the boss. "Okay, but let me get the portable phone first."

I inched my way back into the living room, found the portable and switched it on. The moment I pushed the button, the line went dead. Staring at the phone in disbelief, I knew I had one option. I had to run.

At Super-cuts, my dad stood from the barber's chair with his hair half-cut, handed cash to the stylist, and said he'd be back. He ran out and found my sister and cousin roller-blading near Save-Mart and rushed them into the van. As they sped home, Dad handed his phone to my sister and told her to try the house. All they got was a busy signal.

By now they were all worried. Dad called my mom and informed her that I may have been kidnapped. From there it snowballed, and more people got involved. Uncle James received a call and responded with urgency. He, Aunt Katie, and my little cousin, Rebecca, jumped into their Explorer and headed toward Woodward Lakes to assist in organizing the search. But before he got there, he found something interesting at the corner of Champlain and Perrin, near the Super-Cuts my dad had left ten minutes earlier. On the corner of the street, barefoot and sweating profusely, stood yours truly.

Back at the house, Dad addressed a group of worried neighbors. My sister and cousin were on their knees crying and praying. Everyone was ready to begin searching for the missing kid. The search didn't take long. Before anyone left to their assigned sectors the green Explorer drove up, and the supposed kidnapped George jumped out. A look of relief, mingled with annoyance, spread over the faces of everyone. I hadn't been kidnapped. I made a run for Super-Cuts to find my dad. Somehow, while I was strategically hugging the fence line, in case my likely pursuer gave chase, my dad sped by and we missed each other. I made it all the way to the shopping center running barefoot, giving my dad plenty of time to prepare a search party.

Before I could explain what happened, my cousin, sister, and mother swarmed and latched onto me for several minutes, at the same time cursing me for scaring the life out of them. This really drew the family together.

A few minutes later the cops showed up. They searched the house and found nothing but a paused video game, and the phone left off the hook in the kitchen. They left without speaking to me. I can still picture them laughing to themselves about the jumpy fifth-grader who caused a whole block a half-hour of panic.

Now, the police may have said there was no one in the house, and all the evidence may point to that apparent truth. But even the valid explanation of the portable phone battery out of juice causing the line to go dead, cannot convince me there was no one in the house. Everyone can think what they may; I know I acted rationally. At least that's what I've told myself for the past eight years.

George is eighteen years old and attends college at Pepperdine University. Most of his waking hours are spent playing video games and reading comics; supplemented by occasional homework. But when it all comes down to it, he'd rather just be hiking in Yosemite.

MISSING

By Ben Romero
Dedicated to my son, Gabriel

"Gabe, where are you?"

I was frantic. My twenty-two month-old son had disappeared. What was I going to do? What would I tell my wife?

It had started as a regular Summer day. I watched my son while my wife worked and our other children attended year-round school. I worked in the evenings, so my wife took full responsibility of the kids at night.

How could I let him out of my sight?

We lived in the country. There was only one other house on our block, and a wire fence separated our properties. We spent most of the day in our huge back yard, watering trees, working, and playing.

I searched the hen house, Gabe's favorite place to play. No sign of him. Then a gut-wrenching fear struck me. The pool!. I ran to our doughboy and searched it end to end. Not there. Whew!

Our two dogs followed me for a while, then lost interest and found a cool shade. *He has to be around here, someplace.*

I ran in the house and searched every room, under every bed and inside each closet. The front door was locked, so there was no way he could have gotten out.

Should I call the cops? No. They'll think I'm negligent.

"Gabe! Gab-ri-el!"

No response.

I felt sick. *I have to think. He can't be far away. All he has on is a pamper.*

I sat in the shade on a bench, leaning my head on the picnic table. *Oh, God, help me find him.*

Then I heard a faint snore. I picked up my head and looked around, listening. There it was again!

Right in front of my eyes was a rabbit hutch/chick house. I had cleaned it out and was preparing to put a new door on it. Gabe's foot was barely visible in the little doorway.

In his little mind, it must have seemed a perfect spot to curl up and sleep. After-all, in early Spring that hutch held bunnies. We had often placed chicks in there and watched them snuggle against sleeping rabbits. He must have climbed from the very bench where I sat, to the picnic table and into the hutch.

PROJECT FIREWORK
By Gabriel Romero
Dedicated to my cousin, Marisol Gonzales

I went the whole trip without buying anything but a Rolling Stone magazine and the occasional snack, whenever I found myself without a parent to beg food off of. This was serious business. I left California with fifty dollars in my pocket, intending to bring back as many illegal fireworks as possible. California fireworks follow vigorous safety guidelines, rendering them useless and unentertaining.

There I was in a portable trailer, converted into a firework liquidation center; a proverbial kid in a candy store. This was going to be tough. *Do I get a little of everything? Or do I try to get more bang for my buck? We only visit New Mexico once a year so I'd better go all out. Big bang it is.*
I loaded up my basket with as many bottle rockets and anything else I could find that would go airborne. I also got a much-needed roll of 250 black cat firecrackers to continue my long waged war on the ant colony in my back yard. And there it was. The clouds parted and a bright light shone down on the mother of all affordable rockets.
A box of bottle rockets flew out of my basket to make room for a slick black Night Hawk Nitro Rocket that screamed danger.

Fast forward one month to an explosive Fourth of July. It was my family and my favorite girl cousin, Marisol's family. The bottle rockets red glare, the smoke bombs bursting in air… It looked more like a battle than a safety-first holiday. We lived in a rural neighborhood, so the "Battle of the Driveway" raised few eyebrows. Or did it? The Ranchos Patrol, the rural quasi police, were out in full force. We would see them turn the corner and stop using anything that flew or exploded. I was saving my Night Hawk Nitro Rocket for last, but the increasing drive-bys of the

Ranchos Patrol made me uneasy. *Maybe next year.*

Marisol didn't know about it until I bragged and pulled it out of a bag in my closet. "What are you waiting for?" She teased.

I explained my hesitation which was immediately ruled cowardly. I don't know how she does it but I soon found myself in all-black clothing, with a rocket in one hand and a box of matches in the other. We devised a detonation plan that consisted of going across the street to the elementary school, lighting the rocket, then jumping the fence and running into my front yard, consisting of hundreds of highly flammable trees to hide. Wait. Did you just catch a potential glitch in that plan? We didn't.

The clock struck midnight and we snuck out of the house and ran for it. The middle of the soccer field looked sufficient. We did one last look around and the coast was clear. I lit it and ran for my life, hitting the deck with Marisol like we just threw a grenade. It shot off straight for the moon, leaving behind a furious stream of light gray smoke. As it turns out, the moon was not directly above us that night. The rocket flew straight for my front yard, and exploded in a glorious and fulfilling fashion. It gave out a loud boom and sparks of fire flew like New Year's confetti, but died down before they hit the ground. Except for that big one. The hollow rocket shell itself had caught on fire during the explosion, and fell in a patch of dry grass under a tree made of lighter fluid. I ran for my front yard, but Marisol yanked the back of my sweater before I could. "Look!"

The rocket's detonation had left behind a ring of fire as it's crater. As I stomped on the crater in the soccer field I saw a fire spontaneously ignite in my front yard. As we ran for our lives the second time that night, I couldn't help but feel like a muppet. This kind of stuff only happens to Kermit the frog. We jumped the fence and stomped out our second potentially devastating fire in 15 seconds.

As we began disposing of the blackened rocket leftovers we saw headlights approaching. We both screamed like a rabbit before it dies and hopped deep into the yard, diving under a stack of branches behind some thick trees. The patrol car slowed as it

71

passed the yard, but continued after a brief, yet gut wrenching pause. We ran to the house, locked the door, put our backs to the door to let out a sigh of relief like they do in movies, and turned off all the lights. We had to laugh at how stupid, yet lucky we were. The best eight bucks of my life.

*Gabriel Romero is a third-year student at Fresno State University, majoring in Construction Management. He's working his way through college and spends most Saturdays volunteering his time helping build homes with Habitat for Humanity. Although he is not pursuing his writing talent, he's smart enough to keep his options open.

THE SUIT

By Pedro A. Romero
Dedicated to my mother, Evelyn Romero

I looked into the large bag that my mother handed me and gasped. I shook my head and tried to run away as my father asked, "What's wrong?"

"I am not going to wear that," I said, pointing at the bag.

My father laughed and my mother turned to give me the meanest look she could muster. "You will wear this. No if's, and's, or but's."

"But mom," I pleaded, "It looks like something the Temptations would wear."

"You're lucky she didn't get you a Liberace suit, "my father joked.

I tried to leave the room and my mother pointed at the bag. "Go in your room and try it on. Now. Don't come out until you're wearing it."

I grabbed the bag and sulked out of the room.

I was 7 years old and my uncle was getting married. For some reason, I was chosen to be the ring-bearer and was forced to wear the hideous guacamole-colored suit. It had leather arm-patches and the shirt had ruffles. It was God-awful.

I put the suit on and exited my room. My father pointed and giggled, "I think you got him the Liberace suit instead of the Temptations one."

I started to frown. Tears formed, but my mother, trying not to laugh, came to me with her hands on her cheeks. "Benny," she said, over her shoulder, "leave him alone. He looks like an angel in this handsome suit."

"Looks sure can be deceiving," my father said.

At the wedding, my cheeks were continuously pinched and my head was patted like I was Lassie. Afterwards, we exited the church and I saw my mother talking amongst a bunch of ladies. I walked up to her and asked, "Where is the man with the shotgun?"

My mother looked at me funny and asked, "What do you mean?" The other ladies commented on my suit.

I replied, "Dad said something about a shotgun-wedding."

My mother gasped and shooed me away.

As we came back to the house, I saw people putting up decorations in the garage. It was a typical Mexican wedding, complete with streamers and Mariachis. Homemade food was spread out on a table.

"There are two rules today," said Mom, looking me straight in the eye, "You cannot talk to any adults and you have to keep that suit clean."

"Will there be any kids here?" I asked.

"Your cousin Eddie will be here. Maybe you can play. But remember to keep that suit clean."

I nodded and walked outside. I saw a car coming up the driveway and Cousin Eddie in the passenger seat. He got out of the vehicle and I noticed he was dressed in a t-shirt and jeans. He came up to me and ran a hand through my hair.

"Whoo, you look like Johnny Carson in that suit."

I asked if he wanted to go explore the surrounding fields and he smiled. I knew we would have fun.

Our house was in the middle of a large vernal-pool, with many fields on either side. Eddie and I walked through the waist-high weeds with two empty mayonnaise jars in search of salamanders and bugs. As we walked, I saw a little movement under a large piece of hardpan. I lifted the rock with one hand, my jar in the other, then dove at the movement.

As the dust settled, I saw I had a small field-mouse in my jar. Eddie wanted to see it, so I handed it over. He tossed it in the air and it landed in a small pond. The mouse seemed frightened and dizzy.

Eddie and I returned to the house, entering through the back. I took off my dusty suit and got a roll of masking tape to help clean it off. Eddie played with the mouse as I tried to get all the thorns and thistles out of the slacks. As soon as I was satisfied with my cleaning, we took the jar and headed back outside.

Just as we entered the hallway, the bride saw us. She smiled and asked, "What do you guys have there?"

Eddie said, "Just a grasshopper in a jar."

"Can I see it?"

Eddie held it out and the bride screamed, running down the hall. She slipped and fell on the plastic runner that my mother had installed to keep the rug clean. The whole reception came to a halt as overdressed women of various sizes surrounded her with makeshift fans.

"She must have fainted," said one.

"Her dress in too tight," said another.

At the tuxedo shop, Mother had to drag me through the door. I was crying. She told me in the car that if she got charged for cleaning, I was going to get it. She was still upset about the wedding, but I could see that she was relieved to have it over with. The man behind the counter engaged her in small talk, then took my suit out of the garment bag. He held it up, then looked at me with a slight grin.

He gave my mother some receipts and said, "I am surprised this little guy kept the suit so clean. Most of these come back with cake all over them."

My mother nodded and her mood softened a little. She thanked the man and we turned to leave. I glanced back in time to see the tuxedo man hit the suit with a hanger. Dust flew all over the room, but he just smiled and gave me an OK sign as we left the building.

Pedro A. Romero is Sales Associate for the U.S. Postal Service in Fresno, California. He has a wife and two daughters. His life is busy, but he finds time for writing. When the time is right, he plans to write a novel.

BIG BROTHER

By Serina Galvez
Dedicated to my brothers, Bryan and Steven

In the perfect family, siblings always get along. But in real life, this is hardly ever the case.

"Serina, think fast!"

I turned in time to see the pillow flying at my face, like a guided missile. Too late to duck. The force knocked me off my feet.

"Ha, ha, ha," teased Bryan, "knocked you on your butt."

"It's not funny," I said, trying to catch my breath. Tears of anger formed.

"Oh, look at the little baby," he teased.

My oldest brother, Steven witnessed the entire incident, but didn't say a word. Later he told me he had a plan and asked me to play along.

"Friends is on," I called, turning up the television. Bryan and Steven came in and lay on the living room floor next to me in front of the set. It was one of our favorite Thursday night shows. Within minutes, Bryan was lost in the program with a big smile on his face.

Steven waited for the right scene, knowing Bryan would have his full attention on Rachael. Then he picked up a pillow and said, "Bryan, think fast!"

Wham! Steven hit Bryan full force with a pillow in the face.

"What was that for?" asked Bryan.

"That was for hitting my little sister this afternoon."

"Well, it hurts."

"Oh, look at the little baby," said Steven.

That was when I realized my big brother really cares, and although we often fight, he'll always be there to protect me.

*Serina Galvez is a student at Madera High School. She loves writing poetry and is exploring writing short stories.

BEING TOUGH

By Esther Pérez Martín
Dedicated to my husband, Daniel

I was in the lila (lee-la) tree, jumping from limb to limb. I felt confident and safe. It stood graceful in the summer and barren in the winter. From it's start as a twig (buried branches, really), I felt it had been witness to the best and worst of everything. *This is my friend*, I thought, as I jumped to the next limb…and fell. Splat! I lay flat on my chest, across the sidewalk lines. The wind was knocked out of me. But I did not cry because I was tough. Maybe someday I would be a cop.

"Esther, stop daydreaming." It was my husband, Daniel. "I'll be back as soon as I can. Don't work too hard," he teased.

He was right. No time to think of my childhood. It was Saturday morning and I needed to tidy the house. My little Mague was being baptized in a few hours. I cleaned, wiped, and dusted, then brought out 'old grey', our square shaped vacuum cleaner.

Aluminum hoses spilled all over the carpet, some still attached. *Why don't I ever put it away the right way?* The hose head needed to be changed. I pulled, tugged, and twisted. My hand hurt.

Stubborn, huh? I'll show you who's tough. I sweated and heaved with all my strength, till finally it gave. Whack! The pipe came alive and hit me in the face, leaving its imprint around my right eye. *What a sight I will be at the Baptism! What will the folks at St. Anthony's think?*

When Daniel got home, he asked about my day.

"It was great…" I couldn't say anymore. I started to cry, just like that. Alligator tears, so foreign to me, dropped on my blouse and on the front of his shirt, as he held me in his arms.

"Shhhh," his soothing voice whispered, "It's all right."

I tried to tell him about the vacuum and felt so silly. I could deal with physical pain, but couldn't control the tears rising from deep within. My body shook in his embrace.

"But how am I going to explain my eye at a Baptism? And why am I crying, anyway?"

"You don't always have to be so tough, Esther," he said. "Sometimes you need to cry."

We hugged for a few moments, then started laughing.

For all my worries, nobody noticed the eye.

Esther Pérez Martín is a 20-year veteran of the Fresno Police Department. She and her husband of 34 years have three wonderful children. Esther's passion is writing poetry. She is published in five books: Treasured Poems of America, 1998, Poetry's Elite, 2000, Awakening to Sunshine, National Library / A Whispering Silence, and A Celebration of Poets. She has also done readings at women's conferences and workshops. In all her writings, the main theme is family.

HAPPY HALLOWEEN
By Evelyn Romero
Dedicated to all the mothers who never got thanked

Halloween was always an exciting day for me. As the holiday approached, I'd use my creative juices to create the best costume possible out of items found within my home. It was the mid-1960's and we were a family of seven in a one-bedroom house, so there was no chance of getting our hands on a brand new store-bought costume.

Since I was the oldest girl, I was elected to outfit my younger brother and sisters. Half the fun of Halloween was designing the costumes.

Years later, I found myself continuing the tradition for my own children. Matter of fact, I would dress up with them as we methodically planned our route through the neighborhood. We lived in Madera Ranchos for twenty three years and knew just about everyone. So off we'd go to get our fair share of tricks or treats in our homemade costumes.

Time passes. Life continues. Children grow. Ours were no exception. When our two oldest children, Andy (Pedro) and Victoria were beyond wanting my assistance for Halloween, our next son, Gabriel was still in need of my designing skills, as were our daughters, Rebecca and Olivia.

On Rebecca's twelfth year, she conned her dad into buying her a costume. It was a bright yellow "Belle" from Beauty and The Beast. I pulled up our driveway and saw Rebecca in her store-bought outfit and shook my head.

I got out of the car and walked closer to Rebecca to examine the investment, "How much did you spend on this?" I asked.

"Eighty dollars," he said, quietly. Rebecca continued turning back and forth so the full skirt would spin with her movements.

Now mind you, I've always been seen as the mean parent by my children. Their father, on the other hand, is the one they go to

79

for favors. This was another prime example of why we earned those titles.

I tried to keep calm. "Why in heaven's name did you spend so much on a Halloween costume?"

His reply was a classic father's response. "Because this might be the last Halloween that she dresses up." He was coming to grips with the fact that his children were growing up fast and he couldn't be the super dad that he wanted to be.

Seven years later, the outfit still hangs in our spare closet, waiting for our granddaughters to fit into it.

And no, that wasn't the last time my children dressed up for Halloween. Matter of fact, they still enjoy the holiday and wear their own homemade costumes to friends' parties or while taking their own children Trick or Treating. The funny part is that they still come to Dad to help hash over difficult situations in their lives. And me, I'm still that crabby old lady that just happens to be their mom.

Postscript: The fun never ends. My twelve year-old daughter just conned her dad into buying her an electric guitar, complete with amplifier, computer software for lessons, case, and the whole ball of wax. I came home from a long day of work to be greeted by this latest surprise. Here I thought the set of drums for Christmas was a bit much, only to have it topped by this. When I asked for an explanation, he said, "Don't worry, she's going to make payments to us till it's all paid off."

Yeah, right.

*Evelyn Romero is the mother of five great children and grandmother of four wonderful girls. She is Ophthalmic Clinic Director for InSight Vision Center of Fresno. She is an active member of Holy Spirit Catholic Church, The Fresno Women's Network, The Fresno Hispanic Chamber of Commerce, an The Professional Association of Health Care Management. She is also married to the most wonderful guy in the world (at least in HIS dreams).

SLEEP AND SOCCER
By Pedro Romero
Dedicated to my Mother, Evelyn Romero

"Wake up."

I shook my head and tried to twist back into the covers in an attempt to disconnect myself from the world.

"Wake up. Time for your game."

I tossed and pulled the pillow over my head as my mother called me in a tender fashion. I could tell she was not upset, but she knew I had to get moving. She prodded me again and I stood, barely. I felt like I had just got off the tea-cups at the carnival as I tried my best to remain standing. My mother held me up and led me to the bathroom. She turned on the faucet and I washed my face with cold water.

"Come out and I'll have some breakfast ready for you."

I smiled, but soon found myself snoozing on the countertop with the water still running.

The night before was my dream come true. My mother had allowed me to have three friends over for a Halloween Party and sleepover. I was never more proud as I handed out invitations and told my friends that we would be watching R-Rated monster movies and playing Atari video games all night. My mother had planned a wonderful night of events for us, and I will never forget how happy she looked when all my guests arrived and the festivities began.

First, we had a game where my mother and my little sister hid bags of goodies in the grove of trees that surrounded our house. Spooky music played over our stereo as we hunted in the dark for the treats. During our search, my friend Brad found a pile of horse poop from my little sister's pony. He picked up a large 'road-apple' with a piece of newspaper, and threw it at the rest of us. It hit Eric, and so Eric threw it back at Brad. Then Nate got in on it. I ran, but soon got involved in the melee.

We came into the house with candy and horse poop all over ourselves, but the fun was just beginning. My mother laughed as we tried to clean off all the dried horse manure from our hair in the bathroom. She wasn't mad at us, and I knew she understood boys will be boys.

Then my mother handed out some glow-in-the-dark makeup. We put it on and tried to scare each other when we shut off the lights. It was delightful fun as we hid behind the couches and jumped out at whoever was passing by. Then my mother handed out more candy and smiled at us again.

"Make sure you guys behave. And remember that you have a soccer game tomorrow, so go to bed by eleven. If you stay up all night, you'll be sorry in the morning."

We all nodded, but as soon as the bedroom door closed, we started messing around. We turned on the television and started watching spooky movies. We kept eating candy and drinking soda to stay awake, then we decided to have a video-game tournament. I had just received a game called Laser Blasters, and we were aiming for the highest score. The game was archaic, but it was incredibly addictive. We played for hours.

As the tournament winded down, we noticed that Eric had fallen asleep. I went into my mother's desk and came out with a Sharpie pen. I started to draw on Eric's face, connecting his eyebrows and drawing a moustache. Then we put his hand into a bowl of warm water in an effort to make him pee the bed. He woke up and got mad at us.

As soon as somebody fell asleep, he would try to get his revenge. This went on all night and into the early morning. When I woke up, I noticed that my left eyebrow was partially shaved off and my whole face was covered in shaving cream and drawn on with permanent marker. Soon, we saw the sun rise and we knew that we were in trouble.

"I feel sick, mom." I was trying to do my best sick impression.

My mother looked at me and tried to suppress a smile. "If my eyebrow was shaved off like that, I wouldn't want to play soccer in public, either." My father chuckled in the background.

I groaned and sat at the table as my mother laid a plate of eggs and potatoes in front of me. The food looked great, but my stomach was spinning from the night of horseplay. I laid my head on the table.

"Mijo, you better get up and eat. You have a game in an hour." My mother tried to sound disconnected, but I could hear an "I told you so" lurking underneath the words. I stood and dragged myself to the couch.

My father helped me outside and into the pickup. He told me jokes on the whole ride over to the soccer field, but I was still tired. The coach smiled and pointed at all of us who were at the sleepover as we tried to warm up. We could not concentrate on anything as the soccer balls flew past us.

Then Eric came up with a plan. He slipped and grabbed his ankle. The coach ran out and pointed Eric to a blanket on the side of the field. Eric smiled at us as he limped over to the sidelines. He was asleep before his head hit the blanket.

Nate said a bad word and was kicked out of the game. Brad kicked another player in the groin and was suspended. All three of them laid on the blanket and slept as I tried to stay awake and in the game.

I saw my mother talking with the coach and then he called me out of the game. We were getting clobbered and I knew he was unhappy with all of us. "You need to get some sleep, son. I told your parents you can go now. But to make up for it, you need to show up for practice a half hour early for the rest of the week."

I nodded and hugged my mom. She patted my head and said it was all right.

On the ride home, my dad kept telling me he would take me to McDonalds or Chuck E. Cheese if I wanted. I knew that he was teasing me, because I was so tired and could not possibly enjoy anything but sleep. He kept joking until we turned onto the driveway.

I tried to get out of the car, but my body was too tired. My mother helped me into the house and led me to my bedroom. She helped me take off my shoes, then patted me as I fell asleep. There was nothing like sleep after a night of partying, or the forgiveness of a mother who told me so.

*Pedro A. Romero grew up in Madera Ranchos, California. He is Sales Associate for the U.S. Postal Service in Fresno with a wife and two daughters. He loves to write.

THE COW, THE MOON, AND THE WATKINS MAN
By Ralph Schleich
Dedicated to Kathryn Schleich Schohr and Elaine Evers Wagner

The third grade teacher said, "Class, we are now going to learn about cows."

I sat up straight and stared at her. What a lucky break. We were going to study something I already knew. I was eight years old, living in College City, California.

"Does anyone know where calves come from?" asked the teacher.

Up went my hand. I waved it, anxious to be the first to answer.

"Yes, Ralphie? What do you think?"

"Well," I said, "the mothers go down in the creek and dig them up out of the sand. The calves are always muddy and dirty when she brings them up to the barn."

The whole class broke out in laughter, including the teacher.

Gary Peterson said, "Nah! They don't either."

"They do so!" I exclaimed, putting my fists on my hips. "My grampa said so."

Many years later I shared this story with my sister-in-law, Elaine, and my sister Kathryn.

"Well, Ralph," said Elaine, "I have a story that tops that." She went on to tell how she was in seventh grade in Biggs, California when the class was learning about space, planets, moons and galaxies.

The teacher asked if anyone could tell the class what the moon is made of. Elaine raised her hand.

"Yes, Elaine, what is it made of?" asked the teacher.

"The moon is made of green cheese!"

The whole class laughed.

"It is too," she yelled over the laughter. "My momma said so!"

Kathryn had to put her two cents into the conversation.

"Johnny and I were home alone one day in 1949 when I glanced out the window and spotted the Watkins truck. I didn't want to talk to a salesman. I wasn't dressed proper and knew it would take an hour to get rid of him. So, I called Johnny over and talked slow enough so his four year-old mind would absorb."

"Did you make him lie for you?" I asked.

"Not exactly," she said. "I told him to pay close attention. When the man knocks at the door, tell him Auntie isn't home."

"And how did that work?"

"He said okay and ran to the back door while I hid. But a few seconds later he ran back into the living room calling, 'Auntie, Auntie, the man says you are too home.'"

*Ralph Schleich grew up in Arbuckle and College City, small rural communities north of Sacramento, California. His mother died before he was a year old and he was raised by his aunt Maud. His father and two sisters lived on the family's dairy, where his uncle worked. He attended a two room school until the eighth grade. Twenty-five students were in his graduating class.

In 1953, Ralph graduated from Sacramento State with a degree in Social Work. After serving in the army, he and his wife moved to Madera, California, where he worked as a mortician at Jay's Chapel for eight years. They had two daughters. Later, Ralph served as supervisor at the Madera County Welfare Department for twenty-six years. He has six grandchildren.

ONE FINGER TO FAME

By Linda Vonk
Dedicated to my family

When we first moved to Oklahoma, no one liked us. We were an Air Force family, transferred to Altus in 1957. There was no base housing available so we were put on a waiting list. We found an older house in Mangum, thirty-five miles away. The house had a large living room and kitchen but the bedrooms were the size of postage stamps.

There were three children: myself, Rick, and David. All three of us were accident prone. To make matters worse, so was our dog, Liverpill.

My brother David fell and broke his collar bone at the age of two and had to wear a cast for weeks. He must have thought he could fly like Superman, and jumped off our porch onto the concrete.

Our neighbor had a pony cart he used in parades. He wanted my brother and his friends to ride it at an upcoming event. Rick managed to fall out and the cart ran over him. He wasn't hurt and Mom said she believed God **wanted** him to be in that parade.

My own experience was a bit more electrifying. I was washing dishes and had a radio on the shelf above the sink. I reached up to change the station and knocked the radio into the water. I got a jolt that frizzled my hair, but left no lasting effects. My brothers used to tease that I glowed in the dark when I listened to rock and roll music. Mama'd say it wasn't funny cause I could have died.

Our Springer Spaniel made friends with the neighborhood priest and often accompanied him on little hunting trips. One day she went hunting alone and got bit on the nose by a rattlesnake. She almost died. Being a dog lover, I held her in my arms and cried like nobody's business. The vet lived nearby and gave her a serum that made her well within a few hours. But it didn't stop her from going on new escapades.

One day she came running into the living room and dropped

something in mother's lap. I thought it was a short stick. Mom's eyes bulged and her face turned white.

"What is it, Mama?" I asked.

"It's a finger. A human finger."

Mama tied up Liverpill and called the police. They didn't believe a word she said, but showed up anyway. One of the officers opened the bundle Mama handed him and his jaw dropped.

"It's a finger!"

"That's what I've been telling you," said Mama.

The two police officers talked for a while then asked Mama to turn Liverpill loose to see if she'd find more body parts.

"Nonsense!" said Mom. "That's your job, not my dog's."

The sheriff was called and a search party formed. They combed the area and found nothing. They sent the finger to the State Prison for testing and finger printing. It was determined that a local doctor had amputated it and put it in a trash bin. The garbage was later taken to the city dump, where Liverpill found it.

During the several days it took to solve the mystery of the finger, our dog became a celebrity. She was featured in the local newspaper and everywhere we went, people asked us about her.

We made many lasting friendships. For years my mother exchanged Christmas cards and letters with the people we met in Mangum, Oklahoma, thanks to our dog and a stranger's finger.

*Linda Vonk was born in Texas. Her family traveled wherever the Air Force sent them. She was an office manager until health problems forced her to retire. She's been writing since the 1980's. She's divorced with two sons, a daughter, two grandsons and one granddaughter.

OKLAHOMA WEATHER WITH A TWIST

By Linda Vonk
Dedicated to James, my best friend and life partner

Oklahoma weather was cold in winter. The snow would blow across the roads so strong and thick you could not see to drive. Spring and summer brought tornadoes and blowing red dust.

One summer my grandparents, aunt and uncle were visiting from Texas. We were under a tornado watch, which meant it was time to seek shelter. Warning sirens had gone off.

We had a storm cellar in our back yard, that we shared with our landlord, who lived across the street.

We all got into the cellar except for my dad and grandfather.

"We're not getting in that 'hole'," said Grandpa.

The door rattled as the wind grew stronger. There was a rope attached to the door, that could be held in case of intense winds. My uncle and the landlord held it tight as the wind howled.

My brothers and I were terrified, our arms held tight around Mama's waist. Dust assaulted our nostrils. We could hardly open our eyes.

"Hold tighter!" said the landlord. "The wind's so strong it's gonna pull the door clear off its hinges."

Then we heard a faint cry from outside. It was my father and grandfather trying to get in. They had been pulling on the door. Those big brave men had spotted the tornado as it headed towards us. They had decided the 'hole' was not so bad after all.

The twister did not hit our house, but it demolished a nearby trailer park. Luckily, there were no injuries.

The next day my mother found a snake skin right by the cellar door. We had been in there with a full-grown rattler who shed his skin when he crawled out. None of us ever went in that 'hole' again. We took our chances with the weather.

*Linda Vonk was born in Texas. Her family traveled wherever the Air Force sent them. She was an office manager until health problems forced her to retire. She's been writing since the 1980's. She's divorced with two sons, a daughter, two grandsons and one granddaughter.

CHECK YOUR TRANSLATION
By Veronica Franco-Cook
Dedicated to my parents, Alfonso and Connie Franco

"Ronni, I need approval to cash this check."

I was the only supervisor on duty who spoke Spanish. The bank was busy for a Saturday. I took it from the teller's hand and had the customer step aside.

Looking at the check I had a gut feeling that I'd better call the other institution to see if it was good.

"Insufficient funds," said the voice at the other end.

Being in a rush, I walked over to explain in Spanish that there weren't funds in the account the check was made from.

I stammered, "La cuenta no tiene fundillo."

The customer gave a puzzled look, took his check and walked away. Problem solved. Or so I thought.

Later I spoke to Mom on the phone and proudly told her how I had used my Spanish-speaking skills. When I mentioned what I'd told the customer, she laughed so hard she couldn't talk. I had to call her back later in the evening.

"Don't you know what you said? La cuenta no tiene fundillo means, the account doesn't have a buttocks, ass, watusi." She finally regained her composure and added, "You should have said no hay fondos en la cuenta. Your customer probably left because he was worried what else you'd tell him."

This experience taught me a lesson. In order to not make an 'Ass' out of myself, I'd better learn my language better.

Mom loves telling the story. Sometimes she fondly says to me, "No tienes fundillo (You have no ass)." Other times she says, "Qué tapada (You're so full of it)."

*Veronica Cook has worked in banking a total of 28 years and is currently employed by Bank of Visalia. She and her husband of 24 years, Mike, met at Orosi High School in 1970 and enjoy camping, fishing, golf, and Blues concerts. She has three sisters, a brother, and two beagles (Sister and Mikie). Veronica, aka, Ronni, also worked for the U.S. Postal Service for eighteen months.

Hair Bugs and Brain Buds
By Kenna Morris
Dedicated to every kid who's ever had cooties

My mother had no wrinkles. Even after fourteen hours on a Transoceanic flight from Guam to Portland, she looked perfect. How did she do it? A light blue round hat perched on her black hair, like a flightless bird asleep.

"Hon, you look just like Elizabeth Taylor. Except for the eyes of course. Yours are even better." Mom smiled at dad's compliment, training her twin beams down on me.

Sea water green, her worried eyes gave me a detailed inspection. "Guess this is it." She sighed, handing me the fat wicker suitcase I dragged everywhere. Down the narrow aisle she towed me, her fingers smooth in their glove skin. The seams dug into my palm, making me squirm.

"Whatever you do, don't scratch!" Mom hissed in my ear as we descended the creaky plane ramp. I would be six in two months and was naturally grubby. I scratched and twitched on a daily basis. To *not* scratch when I had a perfectly good reason, did not make any sense at all.

"But mom…" I wailed, digging into my bushy hair and smudging my ridiculously white gloves.

"Shhhhh!" She yanked my arm down in mid-itch. "Don't tell your G-ma about the bugs or she'll never let you in the house."

Was she going to get in trouble with her mom because I had bugs? Were moms afraid of their moms?

"If she finds out you'll have to live in the dog house with Sam." She warned.

I loved Sam, my G-ma's fluffy collie dog. The thought of cuddling up to his soft, warm fur on an old blanket sounded cozy. Sam and me, we could camp out in 'the forest', a stand of giant fir trees behind my grandparent's house. I'd never have to come inside or take a bath, or put on scratchy church dresses. A viselike grip on my little brown arm jerked me back to reality.

"Kina, did you hear anything I said?" I blinked, visions of my doggie campout blurring.

"Uh, huh, don't let G-ma see me scratch." I slipped behind dad and gouged into my scalp one last time before facing my relatives.

" Stop IT! There's your G-ma. Smile honey." Mom gripped my right arm in her gloved talons. In my left, I dragged the suitcase. The wicker squeaked along the polished floor.

"Climb aboard." Dad lifted me onto his lap in Grandpa Nomad's pickup. We drove out of Portland, four adults and me, squashed together in that old Ford. G-ma kept wiping our steamy breath off the windshield every five miles, with her wrinkled hankie. A wreath of blue cigarette smoke floated out dad's nostrils, curled around his head, then flitted out the crack in the window like a spirit. He blew rings, tubes and twirly clouds that looked like sheep. Green eyes glaring, mother fluttered her gloved hands, slashing the smoke sheep to ribbons. Dad squished out the glowing tip with his fingers, then dropped the butt into his pants cuff. He was a tidy man.

"Look out there, Kina. I used to pilot a tug called the Inland Chief, up and down that river." He pointed through the misty windshield. More vigorous wiping from G-ma.

I loved zooming across the high bridges, searching white caps on the broad Columbia River far below. It was like flying. I gripped the dashboard, grinning, asking millions of questions of my Grandpa who, of course, knew everything.

"When are the salmon coming? Will they get up the fish ladders? Oh look, there's three deer! When will they grow their horns…"

"Antlers, kid, not horns. Salmon will be here when they're ready to live in fresh water. Then they'll leap the falls using the ladders when they get tired. By late August their tails will rot off. After they spawn they'll die and the bears'll eat 'em." Blue eyes twinkled around his beaky nose at my horrified expression.

I sat on my hands. I pulled my dumb gloves off and on. I *really* tried not to scratch. But oh, the itching of all those little bug feet dancing across my scalp. I plopped my head on dad's shoulder, rubbing insistently like a very friendly cat. I purred, he laughed.

"What's a matter with that kid, Joy, got ants in her pants?" G-ma was suspicious. "Maybe she needs to use the ter-let? Norman! Pull over."

Mom had a death grip on my left arm, to keep it from wandering towards my crawling head. My fingers were getting all tingly.

I ran to the bathroom, insane to dig into my frizzy hair. I saw a plastic fork on the ground, and scooped it up as I rounded the corner into the stall. Two of the fork tines broke off in my mad scratching. In the process, several occupants bounced down my dress collar. Unable to reach them, I backed up to the corner wall and rubbed and scratched like a bear against particularly satisfactory tree bark. As the delicate pearl buttons popped off my dress, my mother entered, high heels clicking. They sounded like pistol shots. I froze. She glared as a solitary button rolled across the floor.

" Oh Kreeners and Skublatch! You've torn that Sears dress to shreds!" Fishing around in the bowels of her purse, she extracted a most deadly device: THE LICE COMB. Gripping my head in a choke hold, she raked the teeth through my wiry hair, while I struggled. Snick, SNICK, she dispatched several large lice with her predatory fingernails. Twenty out of five thousand. Not an effective method of bug control. I was miserable, but too defiant to cry.

"Oh Glarb! They're multiplying like fleas." Mom muttered. I followed helplessly back to the truck.

Squirming and smiling I watched G-ma, as she plopped a purple lump of venison onto my plate. She glowered at me, fork poised.

"You have to go, AGAIN? Hurry up and don't clog up the ter-let like you did last time." Nothing was sacred in my family, no topic off limits, even at the dinner table. Grandpa Nomad watched me slink off, fork in hand. He gave me a wink. *Did he know?*

Just before dark, we went to the creek to pick black berries.

Covered in sticky, juice, I shoveled the sweet berries in my purple mouth as fast as I could pick them.

"Yer gonna have the runs, you keep gobbling like that. Don't your folks ever feed you? Your G-ma'll be mad if she doesn't have enough to make a pie."

I grinned, wiping inky hands on my jeans and absently scratching my teeming head.

"I can kill those bugs for you, get rid of every last one." My mouth fell open. "But you gotta tell yer G-ma. I sure don't want to be the one to do it. What was your ma thinkin' lettin' you get on the plane with fifty people, with yer head all buggy. Bet most of them are scratchin' now."

"How did you know? Can you see 'em? I think there are some in my eyelashes. It's driving me CRAZY!" I closed my eyes.

His calloused hand tipped my chin up." Don't think they've hatched in there - yet."

He patted me on the shoulder, "Let's go give 'em the bad news, then we'll cut your hair off." Scratching his rooster comb of hair, he chuckled. "Your dad is gonna have a fit, he does love your long hair. But it's the only way."

" Well, better bugs than bowels." G-ma wiped her red hands on her apron. "At least you won't be goin' to the ter-let all the time. What do you need Norman?" She seemed awfully eager to provide any necessary tools of torture.

" Get the scissors and that jug of castor oil." My mother gasped in her dramatic way, like I was having my head chopped off instead of hair. " Now Joy, don't be havin' hysterics, it's just hair. It'll grow back."

That night, five pounds of wriggling mess hit the kitchen floor. My dad picked up a dark curl and placed it carefully in his cigarette pack. Uncle Roger swept up the offending pile and flung it into the wood stove. The stench of melting bugs and hair filled the cabin like a curse. Dad shook his head sadly, lit another cigarette and stepped out into the fresh piney twilight.

My grandfather wasn't a barber, but did skin a lot of deer, so the haircut was even at least. Next, he poured on a whole quart of castor oil. Then he covered it with a rubber shower cap. Oil oozed down my temples into my ears. I made noises like a wounded squirrel.

"Aw quit your bellyachin'. Does it hurt? No. Will it kill everything? Yes." Grandpa Nomad peered over his beaky nose, like a blue-eyed hawk. " Hey kid, it doesn't itch any more does it?"

I stopped sniveling. One, two, three seconds passed… no tickling of tiny feet. I smiled, " Did you kill them?"

He nodded, grinning under his bristly moustache. "Yes, smothered 'em as a matter of fact. Can't get a breath in all that oil. Gotta leave the cap on for awhile. About four days oughta do."

Another theatrical gasp. "Tomorrow is the first day of school. First grade." Mom clicked across the shiny kitchen floor, heels leaving dents in the linoleum. " She can't go to school like THAT!" Her red fingernail pointed at the soggy rubber mushroom sticking to my head.

I was doomed. Tucked into my sleeping bag, by the wood stove, I heard my parents speaking softly in the kitchen.

"Talked to the airport today. There's one seat to Honolula tomorrow night. I'll have to catch the noon bus into Portland if I'm going to make it. Not another until next month." The metallic scrape and click of Dad's lighter rasped against my oily ears.

My mother, sounding somehow both annoyed and sad, whispered, " But Kina's got that horrid cap to wear and on the first day of school. How can you leave now?"

"Because I've got to make a living. No work here, you know that. I'll talk to Kina. She'll understand it's something she just has to do."

I cried myself to sleep knowing I wouldn't see him for a whole year.

Mom woke me up in the middle of the night. Well, it was still dark and *looked* like the middle of the night.

"Look what I have for you." She pulled a huge box out from under the bed, and let me open it. Crackly white tissue paper shrouded the most beautiful blue and white dress I'd ever seen. The FIRST DAY OF SCHOOL dress. Its round collar, impossibly white, was trimmed in blue stitching. Underneath, a pair of black patent leather Mary Jane shoes, so shiny, I could see my dim reflection, rubber cap and all.

"Oh, Mom! For me?" She grinned, slipping it over my head. Dad came in with his coffee, and took me onto his lap. He helped me put on my new squeaky shoes. His dad-smell enveloped me with a comforting mix of coffee, cigarettes and Old Spice.

" You'll be the most beautiful girl in school" He hugged me tight and I believed him.

"I'll call you when I get to Guam. I know it's hard to do this on your own. But I know I can depend on you. Remember, nobody is better than you, bugs or not. And if it comes down to it, and you gotta throw a punch, make it count." He kissed my slimy forehead, not noticing the grease spot I left on his sky blue shirt. Mom and I waved bravely when my uncle drove him to the bus station. I never saw her cry.

" Load up kid." Grandpa Nomad was honking the truck horn, as I dragged along the front walk. "Good Lord, kid, yer not facing a firing squad. Now hurry up." *Sure, easy for him to say, he didn't have a blue shower cap on his head full of dying bugs.*

Courage is a fragile thing. After all, I was the new kid in town with dead insects floating on my head. Within minutes of walking into class, I was the popular freak show. By noon, my resolve was slipping. A big red-headed third grader pulled up the back of my cap in the lunch line. Oil gushed out, soaking my pristine collar, dissolving the last of my control. Whirling around, I hit him in the mouth. Blood shot out of his lip, splattering his shirt front and my blue cap. We were wrestling on the cold concrete floor when the teacher yanked my hands off his bloody shirt.

"Aren't you that little Guameese girl? Gawd knows what kind of insects you brought over. I'm going to call your folks." She wiped her hands on her skirt in a panicky manner.

"Go ahead, Nomad will come and get me!" I yelled, yanking my slimy cap back into position. All the kids in line giggled.

No one came to my rescue.

Though I had to stay the whole day, nobody teased me again.

They didn't sit next to me either.

When I trudged off the bus, accompanied by a chorus of snickers, my Grandpa was waiting. "C'mon kid, let's borrow some Tide from your G-ma and get this goop outa your hair."

In the back yard, hanging over the edge of the wash tub, G-ma scrubbed with a vengeance. It took three washings, but finally all the dead bodies, antennas and oil were gone, leaving my hair follicles shrieking.

That night we lit the burn barrel in the back yard. Grand pa handed me my soggy blue shower cap and said, "fling it."

I tossed it into the flames. A plume of black stinky smoke burped into the air. We started dancing around the flames like crazed Indians, chanting and whooping. Even my G-ma flapped her apron, and mom waved her scarf, twirling like a dervish. My two uncles beat their plaid Tarzan chests, before we all fell on the grass howling. Not amused, Grandpa Nomad stalked over to the cabin muttering, "Never saw such flaming eejits."

" I think all the evil demons are gone from your head at last," G-ma pronounced.

And she was right. My first school year in the "states" continued to be full of exciting adventures. Zeke became my best friend and taught me how to scream down the hill on his sled. I embarked on my career as a storyteller and became the class clown. They didn't believe a thing I said, but always wanted another story.

A PLANE ADVENTURE
By Virginia Herrera
Dedicated to my daughter, Debbie

Several years ago I was on travel to Pasadena, California for a one-week class and had planned to visit my daughter Debbie, who at the time, was stationed at the Navy base in San Diego. My plan was to drive to San Diego on Friday and spend a week-end of shopping and sightseeing.

As luck would have it, it started raining the afternoon I arrived. I picked up my daughter at the base and we had dinner at the Hotel, hoping for better weather the next day. Well, it didn't happen. It continued to rain and we did not see any relief in sight.

So we, or shall I say I, got an idea. "Why don't we fly to Las Vegas for the week-end?"

Debbie's eyes lit up. "Are you serious?"

By 10:00 AM we were on a plane. We had such a good time gambling, laughing, and shopping, that people must have thought we were nuts. Then it was time to leave Las Vegas and go back to San Diego to pick up the rental car and most of our belongings.

We were already on the plane when we were told that we could not leave Las Vegas because it was raining too hard in San Diego and would have to be routed through Los Angeles. That is when I started to worry. My husband would be waiting for me in Albuquerque, and it was too late to reach him. We lived a couple of hours from the airport and he would have left by now. All we could do was wait.

We finally arrived in Los Angeles only to see the plane to San Diego leaving the runway. Now I was really worried, We got on the next flight, arrived in San Diego, reached the rental car and tried to start it so that I could return it. It wouldn't start. My daughter opened up the hood.

"The battery's gone!" It had been stolen.

With only a few minutes left to catch my flight to Albuquerque, we grabbed everything out of the car. Debbie ran to the ticket counter, I ran to the car rental booth and tried to explain that the car had no battery and finally just left the keys with a very nice attendant who said she'd take care of everything. I had to trust her, and so I left. I was the last one to board the plane as they were getting ready to close the doors.

As I arrived in Albuquerque and saw my husband waiting for me, all I could do was to burst into tears. He took one look at me and asked what was the matter.

"Have I got a PLANE story for you," I said.

*Virginia Herrera enjoys movies and sports of all kinds. She played softball well into her fifties. Her favorite pastime is spending time with family. She has worked in the electronics industry for the past twenty-nine years at Los Alamos, New Mexico and has been married to Steven Herrera for forty-one years. They have two grown children and two granddaughters.

RUNNING TWO LIVES
By Rebecca Rodriquez
Dedicated to my mom and dad

"Becky, you're the oldest when Stephen isn't around, so you have to be in charge."

Sometimes I feel Jesus gives me more than I can handle, like that stingy demon they call my little brother.

Let's just say Jeremy doesn't always make the right choices. For example, say my mother makes a pretzel salad, and sets it out to be cut into equal slices, Jeremy goes behind her back and takes some. Afterwards, he lies about it. Talk about walking on thin ice!

A while back, my family moved to a nicer house (roach free!). But when we still lived in 'Roach City', he sneaked in a stray cat in a shoe box. We already had two very healthy cats, but he just had to bring in a stray. A few weeks later, the older cat got sick and started hyperventilating. Jeremy lied about that too.

Okay, he can be funny and make me feel happy while I'm around him. But only sometimes. One day my brother and I got to pass out fliers in my neighborhood. He suggested splitting up. Mom said to stay together because there are kooks out there. But noooooo, my brother had to split up. Next thing I knew, I was getting yelled at, and so was he for splitting up.

"He's your responsibility, Rebecca Anne!" I can still hear Mom yelling. *Uh, sorry to burst your bubble but I didn't give birth to him.* I decide it's best to keep my mouth shut.

When Dad got home, Jeremy got the spanking of his life. Then I was told I have to make decisions for him because he doesn't know how.

"Now sit here and think about it," said Dad.

I went into the shower (which is where I cry so no one hears my pain), and started talking to myself, giving words of encouragement. I can't count on anyone to do it for me.

99

Later, I went downstairs where Dad was fixing a computer.
"What's wrong?" he asked, in a forceful tone.

I burst into tears. My body shook. "Dad-dy, I don - want - ter-grow -up," I whined.

Now, my daddy can be gentle as a lamb when you deserve it.

"Come here, Baby," he said, in a loving voice. "There, there. Why don't you want to grow up?"

I hesitated. My voice quivered. "Because I don't want to deal with decisions or make them for other people. I wanna stay that little seven year-old who didn't have to worry about what other people think or zits and boys."

My daddy held me. "I'm sorry, but that's life, Honey. Believe me, I wish you were a porcelain doll to place on a shelf and say, 'yep, that's my daughter. Isn't she beautiful?' I don't want to age either." He hugged me once more. "Everything is okay."

In the morning I played a game with my little brother. *Better to make the best of life.* Now I'm trying to be seven when necessary. And I know for a fact that Jesus isn't giving me more than I can handle because I'm doing fine running two lives on my own.

*Rebecca Rodriquez is an eighth-grader at Washington Intermediate School in Dinuba, California.

WHO WOULD HAVE THOUGHT, ON THAT DAY…
By Robert D. Nicoletti
Dedicated to my wife, Nancy and our daughter, Juliann

Ever since I was a boy, I was drawn to birds. Duck hunting became a major interest in my life. Furthermore, I developed an enormous passion in the art and craft of taxidermy.

Through the years, the two interests merged together in a cycle. During the hunting season, I feel a great anticipation of romping in the swamp on brisk mornings to fulfill my eagerness to hunt, exercise, and have fun. The feeling is further heightened by hopes and dreams of collecting an extensive variety of North American migratory species (one by one) to bag, eat, mount, and display in my home. This passionate cycle has resulted in a vast network of birds on my wall, whose fate crossed my path.

There exists a particular species of duck commonly called a "canvasback". This bird is much more prevalent on the east coast rather than the west. They are legal to hunt, but because of their numbers, the daily bag limit in California is one per day. Opportunities, for whatever reason, have always been few and far between. It is still considered a privilege to land such a prized bird.

A few years following some formal taxidermy instruction and well into the start of my collection, I was lucky enough to bag a hen (female) canvasback on a lone hunt. It was a thrill to get such a nice specimen. I mounted it in a nice standing pose on a piece of grapevine. The wood piece was selected specifically to accommodate a drake (male) in the future, whenever fortune would smile. And it became a maddening quest. Ultimately, it turned out to be a rather long time before being realized.

While courting my wife, Nancy, I was eager to offer her opportunities to join me in the swamp and experience the joy of hunting. Coming from a hunting family, she was open-minded about going along and seeing the action.

This one particular morning, we found ourselves situated in "Blind #3". This is an island, fifteen feet across, with two cement barrels dug into the ground, completely surrounded by pond water. We had been there since the early start of "shoot time" and bagged only a duck or two. The weather was not especially conducive to lively duck hunting. After three hours, we called it quits and considered it to be a below average or slow day at best.

Not surprisingly, after all the coffee, Mother Nature came calling. No way around it; I needed to urinate badly. There was no recourse but to apologize and excuse myself from the lady present for having to tinkle at the nearby shoreline. The only way to relieve oneself in chest waders is to roll them down to your knees or below, allowing you to wee-wee without stepping out of a warm, dry boot.

All at once, we heard an enormous gushing of wind and wings. I said to Nancy, "Somewhere up there, we have ducks all over us." Looking up, I was stunned to see a sharp banking turn of a dozen ducks or more, whose identity was unmistakable. The bright red and high slope to the forehead could only mean one thing..."Cans!"

I screamed at Nancy, "Mama mia, those are canvasbacks. Shoot!"

Frantically, with both sets of my pants down, and whizzing away, I stumbled and raced for the shotgun a few feet away. It had to be an incredible sight, as I have no doubt I was flopping and splashing in many directions. Nancy was watching incredulously, as I tripped and groveled in the mud, delirious to get to the gun for a shot.

I scarcely had time to grab the gun from the blind's rim and, without aiming, desperately pointed it straight up into the air and let a round fire. It went off as the birds passed directly over the blind. Miraculously, one of the drakes fell from amongst the pack. I yelled hysterically and blazed into the water with my legs bound and attire still down to my knees.

Nancy alerted me, "Your waders are still down!"

I staggered back to the blind, yelping and panting like a lunatic, struggling to get the suspenders back up. For those few moments of chaos, I kept harping on Nancy, "Why don't you shoot? Why don't you shoot?"

She snapped back, "Pull up your pants! Pull up your pants!"

The bird bagged that day had outstanding plumage and was in excellent condition. It was a tough wait, but well worth it. A flying mount was done to compliment the hen nearby.

There are many birds in my personal taxidermy collection. But there certainly isn't one with such profound significance and comical history that could compare with this one. The trophy is still very prevalent in our home, and a constant reminder of a unique stroke of luck, coupled with a hilarious laugh.

*Robert Nicoletti is full-time engaged in the health care profession. He and his wife, Nancy have been married over fifteen years. They have one daughter, Juliann. And yes, duck hunting, coupled with taxidermy is still his passion. Nancy prefers to spend time with warmer, drier activities.

A LOT OF BULL

By Kathy McWilliams
Dedicated to Norman

Two years ago, my husband and I bought a young heifer and bull calf from friends who were moving and selling all their livestock. They were little and cute, but seemed to grow overnight.

"I'll be castrating that bull calf soon," my husband often said. But that's as far as he got.

The calf got so big, we knew we'd waited too long to put bands on him. I finally had to order a special tool, designed for larger livestock. But before the mechanism arrived, we had a problem. We'd just moved our cows to the neighbor's pasture to let them eat down the grass and the bull calf charged the neighbor's young daughter.

"It's not safe to keep him, Kat." My husband reassured me it was best to butcher the calf. Actually, I had no problem with it. Beef is always better on a plate than on the hoof.

I thought the heifer might miss having company, but she seemed happy to have all the pasture to herself. She grew really fast, especially around the middle.

We deliver our pigs in April and raise them through October so we were busy with them and didn't pay much attention to the heifer. At the beginning of September I noticed she had developed a large belly so I finally asked my husband if he thought the bull calf could have been old enough to breed her.

"I doubt it," he said. He took a good look at our heifer. "Well, maybe?"

At that point I really started watching the heifer closely. I could never see or feel any baby move in her tummy but boy she really looked big. A few weeks went by and I noticed that her udders had gotten larger so I was convinced that she was indeed pregnant.

The following Friday my neighbor and I went for our daily walk. Before we left, I went to feed the heifer and noticed more growth in those udders. No milk, just bigger. I tossed out a flake of alfalfa and she ate her dinner as usual.

I told my neighbor, Millissa to come over and look at the udders to get a second opinion and she agreed they looked big. As the sun set and the evening grew dark, we went on our walk. Then we went inside the house to have a drink and talk while the kids played basket ball in the front driveway.

Millissa was getting ready to get her kids and go home when we heard this really loud Mooooo. I realized it was our cow.

We ran out to see what was going on. I grabbed a flashlight and shined it toward the heifer at the back of the pasture. I didn't have my glasses on. The heifer had her head down towards something black, so the first thing I thought was that she was attacking my black cat, Swirley. But as we got closer we realized she'd given birth.

"Quick! Get towels," I hollered at the kids.

The heifer kept her head down, a mean look in her eyes. "Moooo!"

"Don't you hurt that baby!" I yelled.

"Calm down, Kat," said Millissa. "Relax. She's not looking to hurt her baby. It's you she's focused on."

She was right. I tend to over-react at times. As soon as I backed off, she tended to her baby bull calf. It looked just like the one we butchered in March. We were shocked that she had that baby all by herself. I had just checked her two hours before when she ate her dinner like nothing was going on. The baby was in great shape and we ended up naming him Norman (Like on City Slickers). We still have them both and yes we fixed Norman so now he is a steer.

*Kathy McWilliams, a.k.a. Kat, is Secretary to the Plant Manager at Bakersfield Postal Processing and Distribution Center. She is married and has two beautiful children. For fun, she raises pigs and an occasional cow or two. Every fall, she can be found at the Kern County Fair winning ribbons.

Always and forever

By Priscilla Flores
Dedicated to my husband, Antonio, who will always live in my memory

We drove around the corner in search of parking. There weren't many cars near the building where the fundraiser was held. Music played. The sound made me feel like dancing. Cumbia del Sol was one of my favorites; how could one not want to dance to that Latin beat? My friends and I decided to give it a try. If we didn't like it, we would go home. We had already been clubbing and drinking for a while.

The song, Always and Forever drifted in the air. As we got out of our car, two figures appeared around the corner. One of the men seemed to know us; he called us by name. They were in the dark, so we couldn't see their faces, only their silhouettes. *It seems like a dream to me, that somehow came true*, the song romantically spoke. As they stepped into the light we saw that it was Lupe. He introduced his friend, Antonio. My friends stood, talking to Lupe, and Antonio quickly came to my side to speak with me. We talked for a good twenty minutes.

"Aren't we going in?" someone asked.

"The people in there are boring," Lupe slurred, "no one is dancing."

My friends and I looked at one another. It was late. We were feeling the effects of Partying. One of the girls looked like she was ready to fall asleep. My other friend noticed Antonio and I seemed to getting it off, and gave Antonio my number. "We want to go home. Why don't you call her tomorrow?"

The following day, I got a call. Antonio and I spoke for hours. This continued daily for the next couple of months. It was nice. We got a chance to become friends. During this time we never saw each other. I worked during the day and he worked in the evening. On our days off, we somehow never made it a point to meet or go out. I didn't remember how he looked. It had been over two months since the fundraiser, and I had been a little tipsy, which contributed to my memory loss.

I had been bumming around and not taken an interest in doing anything but going out. I had quit my job in Madera and moved back home a year earlier, when my father died. My neighbors had a little Mexican restaurant in Easton, so I worked as a waitress for spending money. After a while, I also worked at another Mexican restaurant every other day or on weekends.

City College was about to start. Antonio had already been attending, so he suggested I return to school. I decided to take one or two classes in between my two jobs. When Antonio and I had discussed our class schedules, we'd decided to meet on the first day of classes. It was cool for an August day, not the typical California summer heat. The day prior to our meeting I had told him what I would be wearing and where I would be sitting. The meeting time would be 2:30 p.m.

I sat on a bench in front of student services wearing a purple corduroy skirt and beige, short-sleeve blouse with purple flowers. I was nervous as a high school girl. My mind tried hard to remember what this guy looked like. As several guys approached one by one, or in pairs, I'd think, *Is that him?* But as they just kept walking past me, my anticipation would become greater yet.

Then I saw him. I thought to myself, *I hope this is not him.* He was walking in my direction, a Chicano looking dude, with a big mustache, black hair, a little longish, with jeans and beige pinstripe shirt, huaraches, and chewing gum like nobody's business. *This can't be the guy I've been talking to; he looks too rough and short for my taste.*

Sure enough, as he approached, he started to smile. I could see he felt my anticipation. My mouth must have been hanging, with my eyes wide open and looking dumb, yet, he still stood there waiting for me to say something. Finally, we said hello to each other, person to person. Although he said he had remembered how I looked, I hadn't remembered him.

As we continued talking, I realized he was the same person

who had made me laugh and given me positive feedback on myself each time we'd talked on the phone.

A few months passed and we became more than good friends; we became lovers. By January of the following year, we set a September date for marriage. Fall is a beautiful time, when the colors of the year are the most magnificent. The flowers and trees with the wonderful reds, yellows, greens and browns add to the romance. We thought it was the most perfect time. How else could we start a union that was meant to be?

Finally, the day arrived; the day that would bond our union. I felt I was ready to take the plunge. I was twenty-four years old and had had my fill of being single. Now was the time to take my life to a higher level.

The church was half-filled; I could see him standing at the altar. I had my mom on one side and my oldest brother on the other. It was time to march into the church. I was petrified. I remember Mom nudging me on.

Finally, I was by his side and everything seemed to be right. The ceremony continued with the traditional Catholic mass. At the time we exchanged our "I do's", the music softly played Always and Forever. My thoughts returned to the time we first met and how that song romantically played for us. We had many ups and downs, just as many couples have, but I strongly believe we will always and forever be the married couple that has proclaimed our destinies.

THE SNOW GLOBE

By Gloria Prine
Dedicated to my sisters

I remember running around a big empty room and the fun of looking down the windows from the second floor. Toni and Linda were fighting over a snow globe.

My oldest sister, Antonia (Tonie) was seven years old. I was five and my sister Erlinda (Linda) was three and a half. We were excited about getting our pictures taken downtown. The studio was located in an area my parents called Barrio Chino (Chinatown).

My mother picked out our prettiest matching dresses, making sure everything was in place. Mom always dressed us alike for special occasions, such as Christmas, Easter, and certain school functions. This went on for years. Even after my youngest sister, Gracie was born. We were called the Gonzalez quadruplets, getting attention wherever we went. Sometimes it was embarrassing because my parents made us sing. I didn't mind too much because I imagined we looked like the Lennon sisters from the Lawrence Welk Show, plus I really liked to sing. Eventually, when we got older and started complaining, Mom let us pick our own clothes.

Tonie was having open heart surgery in a few weeks, and I had overheard my 'wuela (grandmother) Antonia saying something about taking her picture before the surgery. I knew my sister was ill, but at age five, didn't understand the severity of her condition. It was a life and death situation.

The ride to the corner of "G" and Fresno Streets was long and hot. Air conditioning was a luxury we did not have. We lived off Herndon and Fresno, and there was no freeway across town. Forty years later, the building is still there, but the studio is long gone.

My sisters and I didn't mind climbing the stairs. In fact, we loved it. The studio was a big empty room with only a camera, curtains and a couple chairs. As soon as we saw the windows we ran straight to them to look down at the traffic. Looking down from the second floor felt like we were way up high.

Although we were the only customers, it seemed like we waited a long time for our pictures to be taken. Tonie was first. Mom insisted she have several poses taken, which infuriated Linda. At age three, she already had a mean streak.

The last picture taken was the group photo of me, Tonie, and Linda. As we waited for the photographer to set up , he gave Tonie a snow globe. Next thing I knew, Linda was trying to grab it out of her hands. "Give it to me, I wanna play wif it!" she cried.

"He gave it to me first," Tonie responded.

But Linda didn't care who had it first, she started swinging. Tonie hit her back. Then Linda started crying. And because she was upset over Tonie's extra pictures, this was her chance to get even. She blurted out, "They're only taking your picture 'cause you're gonna die!"

I don't know what Mom and dad heard. I just remember Mom grabbing the snow globe from Tonie and giving it to Linda saying, "Antonia, you're the oldest. Let her play with it!"

I was relieved that I was not involved in the scuffle, and that my mom didn't have to scold me.

We took our last picture with Linda sitting in the middle, holding on to the snow globe. Tonie is sitting to her left, and I'm sitting to her right. Not one of us is smiling, and Linda has big crocodile tears in her eyes.

A few weeks later Tonie had her surgery and the doctors gave her a fifty-fifty chance of survival. As it turned out, the Lord was in her favor.

Today that group picture hangs on our walls, and looking at it brings back childhood memories of innocent times and childish thoughts. Linda still insists that it wasn't fair that Tonie had more pictures taken than the rest of us. Sisters will be sisters, just like brothers will be brothers. There will be feuds, but there is always love. I know Linda loves Tonie, and sometimes I feel Linda brings it up to get attention.

Tonie says she remembers Linda being angry over the snow globe and the hurting remark about her dying. She remembers that she was a seven-year-old girl, scared of an impending heart surgery. She was born pre-mature and had been in and out of hospitals since birth.

The best part came after all the pictures were taken. We went out and had Chinese food.

THE APPLE

By Victoria Romero-Delsid
Dedicated to my daughter, Teniah

My daughter, Teniah, had just started attending Kindergarten. On the first day (Wednesday), the teacher sent home a note asking for every child to bring an apple on or before Monday, for a special project they were doing.

On Thursday, the teacher asked all the students if they had brought an apple. Teniah worried about it all day and even called us at work from her grandmother's house that afternoon to remind us to buy one. My husband and I both assured her we'd meet the Monday deadline.

My husband, Justin picked up Teniah from her grandmother's house that afternoon, and when they got home she remembered about the apple.

"Dad forgot to stop and get me an apple and now I won't have one for school," she pouted.

Justin explained he had stopped at the store before picking her up and went to the car to retrieve the coveted apple. He walked in and opened up a bag, showing her a great big candy apple, like the ones you get at the fair.

"No Dad! They want us to bring a regular apple and now I have a candied one!" I saw the fear in her eyes and was wondering how Justin could have been so absent minded.

"Just kidding. I bought that for you to eat. Here's your real apple." He proceeded to produce something else from the bag. And then she snapped.

"Dad! That's a pear!!" Now she was really in a panic. Suddenly the thought of bringing a candy apple wasn't so bad, compared to being the only kid with a pear. "I can't bring a pear. Everyone will laugh at me!"

"What are you talking about? That's an apple," he joked.

"No it's not. It's green."

"Some apples are green," said Justin. "Just take the pear and nobody will notice."

I really thought she was going to burst into tears, but surprisingly enough, she held it together.

"Okay, I'll take the pear," she sighed.

Then out of the bag came two beautiful apples, one red and one green.

"Take whichever one you want, or you can take both in case someone forgets theirs."

I don't know if it was happiness or relief, but I've never seen her so content.

GEORGE
By Victoria Romero-Delsid

After all the hype, the big day finally arrived. It was the day for choosing our next U.S. President and my daughter Teniah was thrilled I was letting her go with me to the polls. She had just turned 5 and I thought it would be a good opportunity to teach her about secret ballots and democracy.

"Okay, now we're going to walk in and I'm going to be voting for Al Gore or George W. Bush, and after everyone in America is done voting, they will count the ballots and declare a winner." No one had any idea there would be the infamous recount that year. Anyhow, Teniah and I walked up to the poll and closed the curtain behind us. I explained about how you punch little holes in the card and so on. Before I could finish my explanation, Teniah gave me a little elbow and a wink and whispered, "go for George Washington."

*Victoria Romero-Delsid is a Postal employee in Fresno, California. She and her husband, Justin, are raising two beautiful daughters. With little time for writing, she's content to read to her girls.

IT'S A HAIR THING...
By Claudia E. Soria-Delgado

This small narrative is dedicated first and foremost to my babies, Reyes and Macui-Xochitl; to Richard for being a great parent; to Julian, Alex and Gaby my nephews and niece; to Maria Guadalupe, my Amá for setting such a great foundation for me; to my sister, Bea and my brother-in-law Beto (you two are the best); to my adopted mommy Rosanna and my Nina Angie for always being such a constant spiritual guidance in my life; to Ann for putting up with me as a parent and for your dedication as an educator to so many of our children, along with taking the time to correct my grammar for this narrative; to mi Ray (thanks for reviewing and giving me such great feedback); to Margarita and Juan Felipe for re-inspiring me to write after being suppressed for so many years. Lastly, I dedicate this to all parents and I thank the creator for blessing me with the gift of expression to write.

I still recall my son's tears and the pain they caused me. He was in third grade.

"Mom it's not fair," he said.

"What's not fair, mijo?" I responded.

"Why do I have to have only one color on my hair? All of my friends have two-tone hair and they didn't have to dye it one color. Why Mom, why?"

I cried with him and held him. Life truly isn't fair when a child feels such pain. As a parent, I felt helpless. My baby thought it would be fun to have two-tones in his hair just like all of his soccer buddies. He was blessed with a very progressive grandpa who happens to be a hairdresser, and so began the two-tone adventure.

His hair went through many phases. It was Mijo's fun way of expressing himself. First, he had no hair, then he grew out a fro with all his nappiness. At one point, he even left a little bit of hair in the very front to look like the famous world cup soccer player, Cerritos, from Brazil.

Indeed the hair thing was the one time when he felt somewhat suppressed. He went to school on a Monday and was informed that he could not have two-tone hair at school. After some discussion it was decided that it would be best to have only one color. He came home and overnight his hair was blonde. Thank goodness for 'Pop,' his progressive grandpa.

I reviewed the parent student handbook with Mijo and did not find anything indicating that a student could not have two-tone hair. However, it did say a student could not have hair that was distracting to the educational environment; i.e. blue or unnatural colors, etc.

I corresponded with the principal via email about the two-tone hair. We live in a time that is truly amazing and it is so great that we can even email the principal. I think she handled the situation very professionally and even thought Mijo looked cute. She was simply doing her job. Regrettably during the process my son's feelings were hurt.

By Thursday of that week the trauma caught up to Mijo. After shedding all those tears he wrote this letter to the principal and she cried too:

"Dear Mrs. Principal,
It's not fair that another kid has two colors on his hair and I can't have two colors. My handbook didn't say anything about two tones. So why can't I have two tones? I'm feeling that it's just not fair because I'm colored and this other kid who is white can have two tones but I can't. I liked my hair with two tones. So why can't I have two tones? I'm feeling very hurt. So can I wear two tones? You need to change the handbook."

We watch our children go through trials and tribulations and support them as much as we can. This experience flourished into a positive. I appreciated the way the administration handled the situation when it was brought to their attention. Mijo was not being singled out. As a matter of fact, once he wrote the letter every student that had two-tone hair was asked to report to the office and was told the same thing Mijo was told. It's amazing what one little letter and some tears shed by all, including the principal will do.

As I reflect on this incident I'm amazed that as a parent, I couldn't have helped him more. Mijo still shares this experience with others and I am pleased that he does not have harvested anger about it. I am certain that he is not the first or last child to go through something like this. I am actually pleased that he experienced this at such a young age, as it has made him a stronger young man.

I am convinced more hair incidents will follow. After all, we're talking about Mijo. I remember that 'Afro Thing' during Volleyball season, then the 'Corn Row Thing'. It only lasted a week because he couldn't stand his itchy scalp. The Hair issues will indeed be a part of our life no matter what.

I love that Mijo can express his Blaxican self by a trim or growth here and there. Simply put, we are a Hairy kind of familia.

*Claudia E. Soria-Delgado is a native of Dinuba, California, located en El Valle Centrál. She is a proud mother of Reyes and Macui-Xochitl. Claudia is a graduate of Kings River Community College and California State University, Fresno. She enjoys amusing her friends by writing poems about their relationships. Her favorite 25 year-old hobby is playing volleyball at least three times a week.

MICROWAVES AND PAUL

By Berta Guerra
Dedicated to my husband, Paul

"Why do we need one?" That was Paul's response every time I suggested we get something new. I wanted a revolutionary type of oven called a microwave.

"We've gotten along fine all this time without one. Who needs it?" This was his second-favorite response.

I wasn't giving up so easy, and in time I won out. Okay, it took a little whining, but so what? Soon, there was a new microwave on the kitchen counter.

He didn't use it at first. Every time he passed by, he'd eye it, like he was sizing it up, then walk on by. But next morning, before I was even out of bed, I heard a distinct 'beep'.

I'm a late sleeper on Sunday mornings, but curiosity got the best of me and I sneaked into the kitchen and noticed Paul was experimenting. He heated his coffee and warmed up a muffin, testing the time needed for just the right effect. I was pleased. Paul was finally entering the modern age.

The following day, while I was at work, Paul got brave and decided to cook a whole chicken. Thank God he took my advice about using dishes instead of metal pans. He calculated a cooking time of sixty-three minutes for a seven pound hen (figuring nine minutes per pound), set the timer, and went outside to tend his impeccable garden.

Two hours later, he figured the bird would be cooked to perfection and cool enough to eat for lunch. But when he entered the kitchen, he found the microwave still running, the plate broken, and a big black glob. The bird was burned beyond recognition. It looked like a heap with long black strings of plastic. My daughter said it resembled the monster in Alien.

What went wrong? In his haste, Paul set the timer for six hours and thirty minutes, instead of sixty-three minutes.

***

117

Recently, our kids gave us an 'over the counter' microwave oven with lots of bells and whistles. I never got to use it. Paul decided to fry beans on the front burner of our stove and used too much heat as usual. He got distracted by our son, who called him outside to look at a flat tire. when he returned, the frying pan was on fire. The flames leaped up onto my beautiful microwave, melting the handle, along with all the bells and whistles.

We now have a plain, small microwave. Paul uses it for heating coffee and making popcorn. But he never lets anything cook for the full allotted time. The screen constantly reads, **"PUSH START TO FINISH COOKING"**.

*Berta Guerra is a retired Postal employee, now working in education. She and her husband, Paul, have two children and two granddaughters. They reside in Fresno, California.

BUNNERS AND BRICKS

By Berta Guerra
Dedicated to my son, Paul Jr.

"Mommy, I can dry myself." It was hard letting my little boy grow up. He stood shivering next to our wall heater, dripping water from his bath. I had always bathed him, then towel dried him in the warmest part of the house. But suddenly, he was trying to become more independent.

"Oh, don't make such a fuss. I'll have you all dried up and dressed for bed in no time." I dried his hair and most of his body, but when I reached to dry off his private parts, he instinctively swung his body back against the wall...and his butt against the wall heater.

"Yaaaaaaa!"

His butt cheeks looked like waffles.

"You burned my bunners!" he sobbed.

"I'm so sorry, Mijo." Part of me wanted to laugh. I held and comforted him.

"Tell me a story," he said between sniffles, as I applied cream to his backside.

I lifted and carried him to his room. "I'll tell you the story your grandpa always told about playing pirates."

"Okay," he said, laying down to hear the story I'd told a hundred times.

My father was orphaned in Mexico at nine years of age. He and his siblings were alone in the world and had to depend on each other. He spent his days on horseback riding with friends. They would grab freshly made tortillas and a salt shaker, then head down to a nearby river to catch turtles.

They'd build a big fire and roast their catch. A warm tortilla, a salt shaker, and fresh turtle meat. Life was good.

After a short siesta, they'd explore nearby caves. One cave in particular, became their favorite. There were moss-covered bricks piled against a wall, up to the ceiling.

Each boy took equal amounts of bricks and set out to build their own fort. The work was hard because the bricks were heavy. They pretended to be pirates and played for hours. Afterwards, they stacked them back up and rode home.

My father came to the United States as a young man and never forgot the bricks or the caves. It was years later that it dawned on him what the bricks were. But try hard as he may, he never got to revisit the caves and what he now knew were moss-covered bullion bricks.

Paul was fast asleep long before I finished telling the story. But it didn't matter. I enjoyed telling it. Perhaps someday I'll be telling it to Paul's children.

*Berta Guerra is a retired Postal employee, now working in education. She and her husband, Paul, have two children and two granddaughters. They reside in Fresno, California.

CRUISE

By Marcella Haber
Dedicated to my sister, Ramona

"I don't want to go on a long cruise, in case we don't like it. What if I get sick?" As excited as I was, the thought of a long time away from land made me nervous. My husband, Mark and I had been talking about our vacation for months.

"We can take the one from Los Angeles to Ensenada, Mexico," suggested Mark.

That made more sense. "Let's invite Ramona and Leroy. The four of us will have a ball no matter what." My sister and her husband are always fun on trips.

I made the reservations for all of us. Vanessa, our agent, helped with the details. We became good friends over the phone. Mark and I scrambled to get all our documentation for the trip, but Ramona and Leroy lagged.

As the deadline neared, they still did not have their documents ready. I called Vanessa and the information on them had been lost. We worked one whole evening getting it resolved.

The day of the cruise, we were excited as school children. Mark and I got up early and went to Ramona's house. Together, we loaded our luggage and set off to Albuquerque airport.

When we arrived at Los Angeles, we went outside to flag down a taxi. It wasn't as easy as I thought it would be. We spread out. Then this little Asian man walked up to Mark.

"Taxi? You need taxi?"

Mark waved us over. "Come on, I've got us a ride."

The little guy walked fast. We got to the curb and he had half our luggage, walking faster and faster, pointing to what we thought was a yellow cab. Then he crossed the street to the parking lot and went half way down the lot to an old gold Cadillac. He opened his trunk. Ramona, Leroy, and I were trailing behind. We looked at one another wondering where this man was taking us. By the time we got to the car, he had part of our luggage in the trunk.

"You get inside," he said, bowing and opening the doors. "Where you go?"

We were all dumbfounded and didn't dare ask questions. My mind raced with wonder. I looked at Mark and he just shrugged.

"I give you good price," said the man, grinning and bowing. "I know best way. Get you there fast."

Mark sat in front. Being the stronger one, we thought it was best in case this guy intended to get rid of us. Some of our luggage was sandwiched between Mark's legs, and some tied on the roof of the car.

The man drove like a maniac, speeding and weaving in and out of traffic. All the way to San Pedro Bay, Leroy had his hand out the window holding on to the luggage. By the time we got there, we were so glad to be delivered to the correct spot and not be hijacked, that we thanked the guy and gave him a tip.

"I look for you when you get back," he said, waving as he sped off.

When we got inside the dock area where we had to register, my sister said, "I didn't bring my birth certificate."

The four of us stopped in unison. *Here we go again.* I could have pulled out my hair. *Will we ever get on that ship?*

As it turned out, all she had to do was sign an affidavit saying she was who she said she was. So much for security.

We had a great time on the cruise. Mark went parasailing in Catalina. We went to a flea market in Ensenada where Leroy spilled a Margarita on my head, by mistake. I'm sure he wondered if I would stay angry forever.

On our last night we received instructions to pack all our luggage and put it outside the door. They have bell men pick it up and have it ready for disembarking. Mark and I made sure we had clothes for the next day and a small bag for the morning. I checked out what Mark would wear and told him the clothes did not match. I suggested he take out a different tank top and put the one he had in the suitcase. I guess he misunderstood and thought I would pick out his shirt.

Next morning we were all ready except Mark wasn't wearing a shirt.

"Finish getting dressed," I said.

"Where did you put my shirt?"

"I didn't get it out. I thought you got one when you put the other one away."

"I didn't know what you wanted me to wear."

"Great," I said. "Now I'm stuck with a topless husband. You can't get off the ship like that."

He suggested I wear my nightgown and let him wear my t-shirt. That was not an acceptable solution, but I remembered Ramona had said she was going to wear Leroy's undershirt to bed and give it back to him to wear in the morning. I called her.

"Did you sleep in Leroy's undershirt?"

"Don't you think you're getting kind of personal?" she teased.

I explained our situation and walked to her cabin and got the shirt. Mark wore it half the day till we got our luggage. It was small and short on him so he had a jacket over it on a very hot day.

When we were in line at the airport, I told him to open the suitcase and get the tank top I had suggested he wear the night before.

"You want me to change here? In front of everybody?"

"No one will even notice," I assured him. I even opened the suitcase and got it out for him.

He took off the jacket, then quickly removed the short t-shirt. Everyone around us applauded.

WAS IT THE CHICKEN ..... OR THE EGG (MONEY)?
By Lisa Fibietti
Dedicated to my husband, Cesare

My next-door neighbor bought 12 chicks as a teaching tool for her four children. Soon the chicks became ladies of egg-bearing age. When production increased beyond household consumption, little Jack, in his signature over-sized T-shirt, was sent around the neighborhood with gifts of beautiful white, brown and light-green eggs.

Fortunately, he stopped at my house first. I got the idea that I could enhance the kids' learning experience by going into the "egg-business" with little Jack, to my advantage! We struck a deal by which he would deliver a dozen eggs every Friday, at the price of....well, the price had to be negotiated with the Mother. I thought $2 would be fair for a dozen fresh, free-range chicken eggs. The Mother thought $1 was plenty, paid in quarters, so that each child could get a "piece of the business".

The following Friday I received my first egg delivery. I had four quarters ready, but little Jack had other ideas, he said: "Could I please have a dollar bill?" Jack had just turned seven. Okay, from then on deliveries were on schedule and strictly on a "dollar-bill" basis. Sometimes the dozen turned out to be nine or ten, but never thirteen or fourteen.

A short time later, one of the children noticed an "anatomical abnormality" and the chicken in question was sent to the veterinarian, who performed a hysterectomy, for the equivalent of 960 eggs. Her egg-laying days were over. "Abnormalities" or disease would be dealt with differently in the future, said the Father. Meanwhile I heard that Jack had to give up his latest dollar bill to his older brother Morgan.

Suddenly and mysteriously, egg delivery stopped. I wondered: was it the heat wave that slowed egg production of the eleven still-fertile hens, or was it Jack, who figured, *why do all the work*, if he had to share the profits with his siblings?

I predict a bright future for that little boy in his oversized T-shirt!

*Lisa Fibietti worked alongside her husband, Cesare, managing a 6,000-acre farming property just south of Fresno for several years.. After retiring, she worked as a bookkeeper for Poverello House for six years, volunteered for Big Brothers - Big Sisters of Fresno and taught an Italian class at Fresno State University for a semester. She also worked for Food Not Bombs, a group that feeds homeless people on weekends at Roeding Park and Courthouse Park. She also served on the board of the Philip Lorenz Memorial Keyboard Concert Series at Fresno State. Lisa's greatest interests are genealogy and her dogs. She is author of a yet-unpublished family chronicle (1819 - 1945), and had several short dog stories published in the Fresno Bee in 'Pet Tales'. She plans to move to Italy in the near future.

THE CAT'S MEOW

By Ben Romero
Dedicated to my daughter, Olivia

Yesterday, I forgot to let the cat out of the garage early. I usually let her out soon as I get up (around 6:00 am), and she goes out to do her business. We don't have room in the garage for a litter box. Yuck.

When I opened the door, she stood there scolding me.

"The cat's meow means something," said Olivia. We've had our cat for sixteen years, and our children claim she cat-talks.

Later I took Olivia to the grand opening of the Woodward Park Library, and when we got out of the car we noticed a big cat poop on the hood of my car, right at the base of the windshield.

We went to an automatic carwash where two people stand on either side of the vehicle and give it a pre-rinse, then brush off the heavy stuff. They each use a sudsy water bucket for their long-handled brushes. One of the workers was taking a break, but I explained to the other about the cat poop.

"That cat doesn't like you much, does he," he teased. "I can take care of that."

He picked up his spray nozzle and gave it a strong blast. The glob flew up in the air, across the car, and landed in the bucket used by the co-worker. It disappeared in the suds.

I feel sorry for the customers who came after me.

CHIRP OF THE SWALLOW
By Chong Erskine
Dedicated to Paul, my husband

Our observations of the world of swallows tell us that they have their own language: chirping. The birds chirp to express their love, joy, fear, anguish, warning, and other emotions just like human beings. We talk, they chirp. Also, in their world, there are relationships, parental love for offspring, trials and tribulations. There are territorial wars. They sometimes become helpless prey. The following story is a condensed version of an original titled Story of a Swallow Family.

Last fall, Paul, my husband, and I hired Fernando to paint our house. In preparation, the exterior walls had to be washed. I was not home and forgot to leave a message. I wanted them to not wash away the swallows' mud nest, but to keep it intact under the eaves across from our laundry room. Needless to say, it got destroyed.

The swallows came back in February and seemed to be looking for the nest. I felt sorry for them. Regretting that the mud nest was washed away, I went to a pet store to look for a replacement, but to no avail. I felt helpless.

A couple months later, I happened to look out the window of the laundry room and noted that a swallow was sitting at the very spot where the original mud nest had been. The swallow chirped as if asking, "Where is my nest?" My heart was broken!

In desperation, I went out to our back yard and dug some mud and formed my own version of a mud nest. Paul and I thought it might not work . Anyhow, we tried. I climbed a ladder to attach it at the very spot where the original one had been. It was dark when we finished.

The following morning, it seemed the very same swallow came back and saw the new mud nest. It was still wet though. The bird chirped and swirled around it as if it were happy and excited to find the new nest. It then flew away. To my amazement, ten minutes later, several swallows flew back to the new mud nest. They chirped and gracefully swirled around it as if they were dancing to celebrate. I told Paul what was happening. Excitedly, we watched them, our hearts filled with joy beyond words.

That same evening, April 10th, two swallows slept on the edge of the new mud nest. It was Paul's birthday and it seemed our birds came back to celebrate with us.

"What a nice birthday gift for you, Honey," I said.

"Indeed," he replied.

*Chong Erskine and her husband, Paul are retired. They say retirement is a wonderful time because they have time to spend together and can share and enjoy their lives at leisure. Chong's book, Story of A Swallow Family, is a full study of birds living in their back yard. Some fell prey to predators and others became victims of other, aggressive birds. Yet, year after year, the swallows return each spring and occupy the makeshift mud nest built as an act of love by the author.

THE ONE WHO WOULDN'T TALK
By Ben Romero
Dedicated to my daughter, Rebecca

At nearly eight and a half pounds at birth, Rebecca was our heaviest baby. The doctor said she was healthy and developing well, but my wife and I worried. Her growth was slower than it had been with our first three, and we noticed she wasn't talking. She'd point at what she wanted and grunt.

We tried everything to get her speaking. Aunts, uncles, brothers, her sister, grandparents, everybody tried.

"Say da-da. Can you say da-da?" That was my line.

"Mama," my wife would tell her. "Say ma-ma." No luck.

When she pointed at something she wanted, we'd try to make her say it.

"Ball? You want the ball? Say ball. B-a-l-l." No luck. She'd point and cry until we gave up and handed her the ball.

Our home was filled with speech. Morning till night we talked to her and to each other. Although we spoke mostly English in the home, there was also a certain amount of Spanish.

When she was three, we went to visit my parents in New Mexico. They tried talking to her too.

"Well, there's nothing wrong with her vocal chords," observed Mom. "That girl cries for everything."

Then one day she said, "bird." I got so excited I drove to the store and bought her a toy bird with batteries.

"Look at the bird, Rebecca. Bird. The bird sings. Can you say bird?"

We walked outside talking bird, when she squatted in our driveway and picked up an oval stone.

"Bird egg."

"Whoa!" I exclaimed. "Evelyn, come quick. Rebecca said bird egg." This was a major breakthrough.

Before long our little girl had a small basket full of oval stones. They became her favorite toy. She even took them to church.

One time she forgot the stones at my brother's house and cried till I called and had my sister-in-law mail them to us.

Then one day, the floodgates were opened. Rebecca started talking non-stop. The one who wouldn't talk became a chatterbox that could not be silenced.

"Mom, make Rebecca stop talking. I'm trying to watch TV," complained Andy.

"I can't get to sleep," whined Victoria, "Rebecca won't stop talking."

"Quit interrupting me when I'm talking to adults," Evelyn warned her.

"Rebecca's singing in the bathroom and won't come out," pouted Gabriel.

When Rebecca started school we got notes from her teacher telling us what a sweet daughter we had. "But she talks too much."

"She's a social butterfly," said her sixth-grade teacher. "I put her on the debate team and she dominated the event."

One afternoon I was in the kitchen making one of my homemade pizzas for the kids, when she picked up the phone and called her friend. The child's father answered and Rebecca told him who she was and babbled on and on for several minutes. I was so preoccupied with what I was doing that it took me a few minutes to realize she was carrying on a full conversation in Spanish.

"Hey, when did you start talking Spanish?"

"I don't know. That's all Lorena's dad talks."

I was amazed. I had tried to teach my other three to speak Spanish, but they always answered me in English. I hadn't even tried with Rebecca, and here she was fluent, on her own.

Now, when I hear her angelic voice in the church choir, or listen to her talking on the phone to her grandparents in Spanish, I smile at the times when we worried she'd be mute for life. This was the one who wouldn't talk.

CHOCOLATE GRAVY
By Shirley Clements
Dedicated to Aunt Maydell

Long after moving to California, I remember spending time on a dairy in Central Oklahoma with my cousins. Theirs was a small farm, with twenty head of Holstein cows, milked twice a day. There were row crops of watermelon, cantaloupe, broomcorn, and a vegetable garden. Uncle Pete and Aunt Maydell lived on the farm with their eight kids. They raised chickens, pigs, cows, horses, and geese. In addition to their own brood, numerous cousins spent time with them, including me. It was an adventure; we all slept on pallets laid out on the front porch. There were never enough beds for us. The pallets were shared with five other people, three at the bottom and three at the top. No mattresses, just a quilt or blanket on the floor.

My brother, sister and me, always begged our parents to stay with my cousins. We got to help with the chores, milking cows, separating milk and churning butter. We also slopped hogs, fed scratch to the chickens and geese and grain to the horses and mules. Whatever needed to be done we pitched in and helped. We didn't think of it as work. It was fun. Our reward for helping was the home-cooked meals my aunt prepared. Even today, the smell of pork chops frying, biscuits baking and potatoes boiling reminds me of rural Oklahoma in the 1940's.

Most of all I remember chocolate gravy. This was always served at breakfast with home-made biscuits. The gravy would be warm, having just been made and the biscuits would come out of the oven, golden brown, piping hot. The proper way to eat this was to butter your biscuits and dip them into the chocolate gravy before plopping it into your mouth. There is nothing as scrumptious as warm chocolate gravy on a cold winter morning. Aunt Maydell made sure we had this for breakfast whenever we visited.

I was grown, married, and had three children before I realized the chocolate gravy from my childhood was almost the same as packaged chocolate pudding. We have had it for lunch and dinner but never for breakfast.   Maybe because I don't know how to make chocolate gravy from scratch and it doesn't taste the same made from a package.

My children have asked for the recipe many times.   I regret I cannot give it to them. They remember my aunt visiting and cooking for them.   She always prepared Chocolate Gravy from scratch.   She just added a dab of this and a dash of that with some cocoa and milk, cooking it until it thickened.   There were never any leftovers.

She was the same aunt that on special occasions fed us Fried Pork Chops, gravy and biscuits for breakfast when we were young.   But that's another story.

TURTLENECK TRAUMA

By Lila Pacheco

Dedicated to my mom, Marcella for always making my life so interesting, and to my husband Duane who always listens to my childhood stories and laughs

When I was eight years old, my mom, Marcella, used to get hand me downs for me from my older cousins. A lot of the clothes were great and I was always happy to receive whatever was sent to me.

When the clothes would arrive, it was like going shopping. We would rush open the bags and spill the clothes onto the floor so I could pick and choose what I liked.

A fashion show always followed. I would primp and preen, walking around like a peacock through the hallway, showing off whatever I thought looked best on me.

One evening I was looking through the clothes and found a turtleneck sweater. It was black or maybe red. I am not sure but it caught my eye. I don't think I had ever owned a turtleneck before and I know that all my friends had at least one. I wanted one too. I asked Mom to hand it to me so I could try it on.

Big mistake! I put the sweater on without an issue. I turned and looked at myself and I looked awful. The turtleneck was too small. It clung to every part of my body making me feel like I was wearing a second skin. The worst of it was the sweater made me feel like I was choking to death. I was sad. I really wanted a turtleneck. Here was my opportunity and it just didn't fit right. So disappointed, I took my arms out of the sweater and that is when it happened..

I couldn't pull my head out of the neck hole. I pulled on the sweater and nothing. I pulled again and I was still stuck. I started to yank on it and scream. My mom tried to grab me to pull off the sweater. She yanked. I screamed.

Now here is the deal with Mom: she is determined, as I am sure most mothers are when it comes to a mini-crisis. So when I say "yanked on the sweater," I mean pulling like her life depended on it. I continued to panic and scream. I thought I was going to have to be sliced out of the sweater. I was having visions of going to the hospital half-naked and having a nurse hold me down while the doctor cut me out of this awful turtleneck sweater. I freaked out and got up, off the floor. I got away from my mother and ran like crazy for the hallway, screaming like a banshee. At this point I was also crying my head off.

My dad was sitting in the living room when I burst out of my bedroom screaming and crying. Here I am with a sweater bunched up around my neck, empty arms flailing about and I am running for my life.

Just then my father jumped up and grabbed me. My mom came running behind me screaming at me to calm down. I of course wouldn't listen and continued to have a breakdown. Dad pulled me one way while my mother pulled the sweater. This took several tries. Nothing ever happens on the first try, you know.

Finally after what seemed like forever, I was free!

That night I realized I should never again put on anything that could get stuck around my neck. I never even thought about wearing one again until I was almost graduating high school.

It just goes to show, even a harmless sweater can cause lasting trauma.

*Lila Pacheco was born in Española in 1975 and has decided to make New Mexico her permanent home. She recently married Duane Pacheco of Taos, New Mexico. Lila is the daughter of Marcella (Romero) Haber and has one sister, Kaiwee (Lisa) Wolf Martinez. Lila is currently studying toward her Business Degree, while working full-time in Los Alamos.

THE NICKEL

By Delia Romero

Dedicated to my children: Ramona Roybal, Virginia Herrera, Eluid Romero (Louie), Marcella Haber, Benny Romero, Johnny Romero, and Joseph Romero

Once a year my daddy gave each of us a nickel to spend on anything we wanted. My brother Charlie and I held on to our precious coins for just the right moment.

"What are you going to buy with your nickel?" Charlie was excited about our upcoming trip to Santa Fé. Daddy was home from his job as a sheepherder and had just gotten paid. Supplies were low, so we knew a trip to town was eminent.

I hung my head. "I can't find my nickel."

"Where did you put it?" asked Charlie.

"I buried it and marked it with a stick, but it's lost." Tears flowed from my eyes.

"Did you tell Mama?"

"Yes," I sniffled. "She said I shouldn't have buried it."

I didn't tell my brother the reason I hid it was because I was afraid he'd steal it.

In 1933 the forty mile trip to Santa Fé took two days by wagon over unpaved roads. None of our neighbors owned automobiles and neither did we.

I helped Mama pack food: beef jerky, tortillas, eggs, potatoes and corn. Charlie helped Daddy fill the water barrel and grain sacks for the horses. We left at the crack of dawn.

We stopped to rest and water the horses at Española. Mama said grace before we ate a light lunch, then lay on a blanket next to Daddy. Charlie and I skipped rocks in the chocolate-colored water of the Rio Grande.

"What will you buy with your nickel?" I asked. "Dulces (Candy)?"

"I haven't decided," he said, avoiding my eyes.

The afternoon breeze felt good when we reached Pojoaque. Other families were already preparing their campsites at the gathering place. Children ran in all directions, some splashed in the Nambé River.

While Daddy fed and watered the horses, Charlie filled our canteens with fresh water. Mama and I made a fire and unloaded cooking utensils. I peeled potatoes and tried not to think about my lost nickel. I had planned to buy a double scoop chocolate ice cream cone.

"Levántense (Get up)." Mama's voice shook me awake. From where I lay on the back of the wagon, stars were still visible in the summer sky. Low voices and the clatter of coffee pots disturbed the silence.

While Daddy removed the hobbles from our horses and hitched the wagon, Mama and I prepared breakfast. Charlie gathered our belongings and rolled our blankets.

We stopped to rest at Camel Rock. Charlie wanted to climb the camel hump, but Daddy said there was no time. We had to keep moving so we could reach the top of Tesuque Hill, at the edge of Santa Fé, before dark.

Our time in town was brief, but memorable. Mama bought material and thread to make clothes, and canning jars to store our year's harvest. Daddy bought salt licks for the animals and garden tools.

Our final stop was the grocery store. Our wagon creaked under the weight of sacks of flour, sugar, and rice, followed by tins of coffee, baking powder, and tobacco.

I looked around. Charlie was gone.

"He must be spending his nickel on candy," I said aloud. My throat felt swollen.

Then out of the corner of my eye, my brother appeared, holding a double scoop chocolate ice cream cone.

"Apúrate, Hermanita (Hurry up, little sister)" he said. "Help me eat this before it melts."

LUCKY FIVE
By Delia Romero
Dedicated to my late brother, Charlie Maestas

When I was ten, my daddy killed a rattlesnake near our haystack. My brother, Charlie and I watched in awe, as Daddy ran a pitchfork through its throat.

"Someday I'm gonna kill me a rattler," said Charlie, "and I'm gonna cut off the rattles."

"¿Pa' qué (What for)?" I asked.

"They're good luck," he said. "Anybody who kills his own snake and saves the rattles will be lucky for as many years as the number of rattles. Besides, if I put them in my guitar, it will make the best sound ever."

My brother was two years older than me and wise about such matters.

One day Daddy hitched the horses to the wagon so we could go visit relatives. My brother and I begged to stay home.

"Delia can play outside while I practice my guitar," pleaded Charlie.

"Just don't leave the yard," cautioned Mama.

We had a rope swing in the front yard, suspended from an ancient cottonwood. It was my favorite place to play.

While my brother went inside, I wandered over to the swing. Near the base of the tree I spotted what appeared to be a coiled length of rope. I stepped closer and it moved, emitting a gourd-like sound. I stopped and stared, then turned and raced to the haystack. Daddy's pitchfork leaned against the fence.

When I stabbed the snake, it curled itself around the spikes. I lifted the heavy pitchfork, snake and all, and stuck it deep into the tree trunk.

The struggle lasted several minutes. The angry tail shook with a menacing rattle, as the fat body slithered around the pitchfork handle.   It finally went limp and dangled like a rope.   Closer inspection revealed a metal spike pierced the rattler's head.

I used Daddy's hatchet to chop off the tail.

Proud and excited, I ran in the house.

"Charlie, mira (look)!" I'm gonna have five years good luck! I killed a vibora (rattler) with five cascabeles (rattles)."

My brother's jaw dropped. His eyes looked like half-dollars.

"Let me have the cascabeles for my guitar."

When Mama and Daddy got home I ran outside holding my prized rattles.

"Look at the tree!" I called. "I killed a vibora with the orquilla (pitchfork). I'm gonna have five years good luck."

What I got was five lashes on my nalgas (buttocks) with a tree branch.

"You're lucky I'm not giving you five more," said Mama.

*Delia Maestas Romero was born in Chilí, New Mexico in 1923. Her parents, Eliseo and Dolores Lovato Maestas had seven children. In 1943 Delia married José Manuél Romero of Nambé. They raised seven children. Delia resides in Lyden, New Mexico.

SINK OR SWIM
By Johnny L. Romero
Dedicated to my brother, Benny and my sister, Marcella

I was only 6, but I knew what I wanted. And on this particular day I wanted to go swimming. My brother and sister were arguing in the kitchen. Neither one of them wanted to watch me. Marcella was the one in charge, so Benny really had little choice. I stood in the hallway with a towel in my hands, listening to them fight.

"If you want to go swimming so bad, take Johnny with you," said Marcella.

"What if he drowns or something?" countered Benny. "Mom will be mad at me forever. Besides, yesterday he threw David's model car in the dirt and ruined the new paint job. He's not going to want Johnny tagging along."

"Then stay home," said Marcella.

The pool smelled like Clorox bottles. It stung my eyes, even before I got in. My brother tried to show off to the girls by going straight to the diving board. He hopped at the edge and bounced like a bullfrog. I imagined he could catch flies with his tongue if he wanted to. The girls didn't take a second look at him.

"Go to the shallow side," called Benny, pointing to an area full of kids. "This part is only for people who can swim."

"I know how to swim," I said under my breath. I'd practiced in the acequia (irrigation ditch) behind Grandpa's house many times. All you had to do was move your arms like a bird and keep your head above the water.

I pretended like I was going to the child section, but as soon as Benny looked away, I hurried to the deep side and jumped in, flapping my arms. Water rushed into my mouth and nostrils. I started to sink. My eyes stung.

From out of nowhere a hand wrapped around my neck and pulled me to the surface. I turned and grabbed my rescuer with both arms, gasping for air.

"You're going to drown me," sputtered Benny, trying to shake me loose. He got hold of the ladder and both of us climbed the steps.

A shrill whistle sounded and a dark lifeguard scolded us.

"What are you two doing on this side of the pool?"

"I told him to stay on the shallow side," Benny explained.

"Both of you stay on that end," said the guard. It was no use arguing. Teenagers pointed at us and laughed, even David.

"Now look what you did," scolded Benny.

"Why'd you pull me up?" I asked. "Couldn't you see I was swimming under water?"

*Johnny L. Romero was born in Nambé, New Mexico in 1960. He has three brothers, three sisters, and two grown sons. He is a truck driver by trade.

FLASH FIRE

By Joseph L. Romero
Dedicated to Karen

"You should change those pants," said Karen.

"Why? They're clean." I knew she was making reference to my expanding waistline. I'd saved my dressy black pants for special occasions and hadn't realized how long it had been since I last wore them. Minutes earlier I'd thought of changing, but not now. Maybe I'm too stubborn.

Karen looked nice. The heavier I got, the thinner she got. *What's the big deal? We're just going to town.*

"Did you remember to wash the truck?" asked Karen.

"No. I told you we're taking Marcella's car. She wants me to listen to a noise it's making."

My sister handed me the keys and told us to enjoy the movie. We needed to get out more often without the boys. As we turned to leave, she said, "Couldn't you find a tighter pair of pants?" I ignored the comment.

The car ran good. We drove the fifteen miles to Española without a problem. The sun was giving way to evening shadows. I turned on the headlights. Then I smelled something electrical. A thin line of smoke appeared from under the dashboard.

"Smoke's coming out from under the hood!" Karen's eyes widened.

I pulled over and parked in front of a car lot. Both of us jumped out. I opened the hood and black smoke gave way to tall flames.

I pushed Karen away. "Get back!" I scooped dirt with both hands and poured it on the fire. I wished I had a jacket or blanket to smother the flames. Cars slowed down and people stared, but nobody stopped.

Finally, after bending down several times to scoop dirt, the fire was put out. A lady walked over from the car lot, handed me a

141

small blanket, and walked away.

"That woman's an idiot," I told Karen. "She waits till the fire's out, then she hands me a blanket."

"I don't think it's for the fire," said Karen, with a wide grin. "Look at your pants."

The back was ripped from end to end, exposing my underwear.

*Joseph L. Romero lives in Lyden, New Mexico, where he rebuilds appliances for a living. He and Karen have three boys: James, Manny, and Louis Romero.

SOMETIMES CHICKEN AND SOMETIMES FEATHERS
By José Manuél Romero
As told to his son, Ben Romero

Growing up, I spent most of my time with Papá. I especially enjoyed horseback trips to the mountains, where we grazed livestock.

I was 10 years old when my brother, José Simón, was born. Papá decided we should bring home a cow to supplement the milk needed for the baby. Before we left, Mamá made me a new pair of moccasins. This did not sit well with my 9 year-old brother, Willie.

"Why do you get new shoes and not me?"

"Aveces gallina y aveces plumas (Sometimes you get chicken and sometimes feathers)," I responded.

We took a packhorse for our supplies. Papá used a saddle, but Willie and I rode bareback. Willie's mount was not fully trained, and gave him trouble from the start.

"Why do you get the good horse while I'm stuck with this wild mustang?"

"Sometimes chicken and sometimes feathers," I responded.

Papá unpacked carne seca (beef jerky), elotes (ears of corn), potatoes, and chile. He cooked stew while Willie and I hobbled the horses and set out our blankets. We always picked a spot near one of four springs on our route, along the Sangre de Cristo Mountains. The village of Nambé was visible below.

Papá woke us at first light. He poked the fire and filled the blackened coffee pot with spring water. My brother and I grabbed our rope bridles and set off to get the horses.

Mine was easy to approach. I removed the hobbles and easily slipped on his back. Willie's horse shied away, hobbling out of reach. It looked so funny, I decided to make the most of it. Next time Willie got close to his mount, I galloped my animal close to his, waving my arms. Willie's horse spooked and tried to run. It tripped and fell on its side.

"Stop it!" cried Willie.

"Okay, okay. Go get him," I laughed.

Willie talked to his mustang in a soothing voice and finally got close enough to touch him. I decided to spook it again, and ran my horse toward him, waving my arms as before. My mount stepped wrong, lost its balance, and sent me flying. I landed face down, crushing my right arm. The pain was unbearable.

Next thing I knew, Papá was tying a sling around my arm, scolding as he worked. The bone was broken in three places. It never healed right and eventually kept me out of military service during World War II.

On the way home I rode double with Papá. Willie rode my horse, leading his own. When we stopped for water, I stepped in the stream and soaked my new moccasins. As the sun grew hot, my shoes got so tight I couldn't wear them.

The sun was setting when we turned the corner and our house appeared. Willie complained that he was hungry, hot and tired.

"At least you have shoes," I grumbled.

He responded by throwing my own words back at me. "Sometimes you get chicken and sometimes feathers."

*José Manuél Romero was born June 7, 1924, in Nambé, New Mexico. He married Delia Maestas in 1943, and together they raised four sons and three daughters. He died on June 18, 2003.

EVERY CHICKEN HAS ITS DAY
By Victoria Romero-Delsid
Dedicated to Whitie's memory

"Daddy, how do you choose which chicken you're going to kill today?" It was an honest question from a six year-old's perspective. I didn't have much of a sentimental connection with the majority of them because I didn't view them as pets. We did raise a few with the agreement that Dad would not slaughter them without our permission.

"Well, look at this one. She's old and her meat will be tough," he said, while holding a white chicken I called Whitie. I saw a hint of sadness in his eyes as he explained that she didn't lay eggs any more but could be useful as chicken soup. In other words, her day had come.

I sat and watched the whole production, as usual. My brother, Andy never had an interest in it, but to me this ritual was absolutely fascinating. It held my attention like fireworks on the 4th of July. The only one who shared my attention span was our cat, Red. But I sensed he only stuck around for the gizzards.

First, my father knocked the chicken out with a wooden club, "so she won't suffer," he said. Then he laid her down and smoothed her feathers a little. I was mesmerized as I watched him grab the axe and WHACK! He chopped her head right off.

That was always the best part, watching their heads bounce all over. Sometimes their bodies would get up and run around without the head. On this day there was no fun to be had because I kept thinking that if Whitie had laid just one more egg her head wouldn't be quivering in our back yard.

Red licked his chops as we watched Dad wire Whitie's feet to the fence and begin plucking. How odd. Underneath the feathers, Whitie looked just like any other dead chicken.

As Dad started pulling out the guts, he turned and gave me a shocked look. I thought he was going to play a trick on me to lighten my mood, like pretending that his hand was stuck inside the chicken or chasing me with the guts. To my surprise, Dad pulled out a perfectly formed egg from inside Whitie. It was bright white and I begged Dad to let me eat it.

"If you take the chicken inside and cut it up for dinner you can eat the egg." There was always a bargain with Dad, nothing was ever free. I reluctantly took the naked bird and muttered, "Why couldn't you have laid that egg a little sooner, you stupid chicken."

DADDY'S BOOTS
By Victoria Romero-Delsid
Dedicated to my daddy, Ben Romero

It was a cool, refreshing September morning. I had worked all morning processing mail until my body felt heavy and worn out. I looked forward to break time, knowing nothing would taste better than an ice cold Pepsi from the vending machine.

I made my way into the break room, dragging, as if to preserve energy for that desperate quest in my pocket for change. It was at that precise moment it hit me; a scent. It was the smell of shoe polish. All at once I was taken back to familiar winter evenings, when my father would polish his boots. He'd use a little tin and brush as I watched his every move and studied every detail of his technique.

Once satisfied with the shine, he'd set them on the fireplace ledge so they'd be ready for church the next morning. The smell of polish never lingered as long as I wished it would. But I knew that next Saturday Dad would be sitting in the same spot and I could enjoy it all over again.

Sunday mornings were filled with masses and homilies, but also with a daughter's beaming pride at how wonderful her daddy's boots looked. My smile would be ear to ear and I just wanted everyone to notice how sleek and shiny they were.

Eventually, like all things, the boots wore out and were discarded. But they will always be as sleek and shiny as ever in my mind's eye.

I paused for a moment savoring the memory, then noticed a mail carrier was polishing his shoes on the way to his route. I stopped and summarized my story, but it was like trying to describe the sunrise. It's never as sweet secondhand.

THE DAD
By Victoria Romero-Delsid
Dedicated to my dad

My father always had a way of teasing my mother. Sometimes it was by tickling her to the point where she'd fall off the bed, other times by calling her "Alvin" instead of Evelyn. But by far the most entertaining teasing was when he'd sing this one particular song..."I'm the dad of three ugly daughters." Except he pronounced the ugly more like Oh-glee. Boy, would my mother get irritated. She would insist she didn't have any ugly daughters and that all her girls were beautiful. Then Dad would try to busy himself doing little chores in the kitchen.

It would start again as a little hum, then a mumble, and before we knew it he was belting out the song again. All I remember is that one verse, but the reaction Mom would give made it one of Dad's most memorable tunes.

*Victoria Romero-Delsid is a Postal employee in Fresno, California. She and her husband, Justin, are raising two beautiful daughters. With little time for writing, she's content to read to her girls.

147

FOOTPRINTS IN MY HEART

By Gina Shaw
Dedicated to Russ. I thank God you dialed the wrong number.

It was New Year's Day 1992 - the year I turned thirty. My biological clock was ticking way too loud. I sat at my dining room table pondering the night before. Well, Mr. Right was not any place that I was at - that's for sure. *Mr. Right and I seem to be on very different paths. Maybe he doesn't hang out at bars or health clubs.*

The song by the Moody Blues, "I know You're out there Somewhere" could be the theme of my life up to that point. I know you (Mr. Right) are out there somewhere, somewhere...I know I'll find you somehow.... And somehow I'll return again to you. As if Mr. Right was out there looking for me, too. I felt like I was searching and searching for Mr. Right without much success. I had many long-term relationships that ended after a few years.

As I sat at the dining room table, I started to worry that maybe I was meant to be by myself. Maybe I wasn't meant to share my life with someone else. I was painting an acrylic painting of footprints in the sand. I always loved the poem and thought I could make a colorful painting of footprints using sand in my paint and then taking the heal of my fist to make the footprint. I was good at making these on the steamed up car windows when I was a kid.

As I made my first footprint, I talked with God about the night before and all the relationships I have had that didn't work out. I asked him for help. "Please let me know when I meet that right person. Give me some kind of sign, so I know that it is really him." Just as I made the first print, the phone rang.

Before I could answer it, the answering machine (which was in a different spot than the phone) picked up. I hurried to the phone, said, "Just a minute" and ran back to turn off the answering machine. I got back to the phone and said, "Hello!" The voice on the other end asked for some guy - I think it was

Jeff. I said, "No I'm sorry you must have the wrong the number" and I hung up. I went back to my painting and got my hands full of paint. A minute later the phone rang again. The answering machine picked up before I could get to the phone. I got to the receiver and said, "Just a minute!" I went and turned off the answering machine and came back to the phone.

The voice on the other end said, "Oops, I did it again."

I asked, "What number are you calling?" The voice said my number. I said, "You're dialing the right number."

The voice said, "I was trying to call my friend to wish him a Happy New Year and I had seen him around Halloween after he moved. I must've wrote his number down wrong."

I thanked him for not hanging up on me, so that way I knew it was a wrong number and not a prank call. I had been getting prank phone calls at the time.

He said, "I work at Marquette University in their Public Safety Department, and deal with a lot of women who get prank phone calls, so I know how annoying and scary that can be." I thanked him again.

Somehow we got to talk and he said he lived around Mount Mary College. At the time, I delivered mail around there, so I asked him what his ZIP code was. It could have been the one that I worked at or a different one in the area. He said, "53222."

That was the one I worked at, and that got us talking some more. He told me that he lived around 86 and Center. I tried to describe who I thought his mail person was. We probably talked for about ten minutes.

Finally he said, "Well, I guess you can say that I have an advantage over you, since I have your number. Since we've talked for awhile I'll give you my number. If you're interested in talking again, great, if not no problem."

When we hung up, I called his number to verify that no woman answered the phone. He said he wasn't married and was at work. I got his answering machine and left a message that I was making sure that he gave me the right info. That left the ball in his court to call me that night, which he did. We talked for quite some time.

The next day at work, I waited until the mail was up in the letter cases. I went over to Gary, the letter carrier for that area, and asked if he had a Russ on 86th Street. We had only told each other our first names. We found a Russell Shaw on 86 Street. Luckily, there were no other Russ's on that street, so I took a chance and sent him a Happy Day After New Year's Note. Imagine the look on this guy when he gets home that day and finds out that the person he talked with last night now knows where he lives?

It really is exciting getting to know someone without the physical attraction getting in the way. You can get to know more of what is in their soul. Granted, the person on the other end could be lying about everything they are saying. In my case God was watching over me. We talked for a few more days and decided to meet in a public place.

We decided to meet on a Saturday night, when we both had plans with our friends afterward. That way, we didn't put either of us on the spot - we could leave and never talk to one another if we didn't like what we saw. We planned to meet inside Mayfair Mall, by Boston Store.

At the time, there was a shop, called Pen & Pad that had a window overlooking the front of Boston Store in the mall. I got there a few minutes early and looked to see if any weirdoes were hanging out in front. I didn't see anyone standing around. Then it was time to go meet. I went and stood there for a few minutes. As I waited, I remembered I needed to talk with my girlfriend, Julie, who I was meeting later that night. I went to the phones, which were off to the side of Boston Store.

In the meantime, here comes Russ. We had described what we looked like to each other, but you don't know if someone is telling the truth about their looks. As I was on the phone, he walked up to another woman standing there who was my same height and had my hair color. He said, "I'm sorry, I'm a few minutes late."

The woman looked at him with a weird look that said, " Why are you talking to me - I have no idea who you are."

He saw that look and said, "You're not Gina are you? I am

meeting someone here."

She said, "No, but that girl on the phone over there was standing here, maybe that's her."

He said, "No, I'll just wait here."

When I got off the phone, there was a guy who fit the description. I went over to him and it was Russ. We had a soda, talked and then went to meet our friends. He wore a sweater that really brought out the blue in his eyes.

We dated and less than two years later were married on a cruise ship. A few years later I looked at the painting I had made that day. I realized that God had provided me with a sign. Maybe it wasn't a sign, but he was carrying me that day as I painted Footprints in the sand. It just so happens that just as in the poem, I only painted one set of footprints. At the time I wasn't even thinking that he was carrying me. I was only limited on the space my canvas provided for the size footprints my hands could make. The Moody Blues song still plays in my mind. I knew he was out there somewhere. I knew that somehow, someday, we would meet. I finally found my Mr. Right.

*Gina Shaw works for the Postal Service. She resides in Mukwonago, Wisconsin with her husband, Russ (Mr. Right), their wonderful daughter Kylie, and dog, Zoë.

DEERFOOT AND BEAR

By Mr. Bear
Dedicated to Deerfoot, who taught me the value of family

My name is Mr. Bear. I am Native-American. I've had my ups and downs fighting drugs and alcohol. But through my life I have met many people. The person I like to talk about is Deerfoot. I met him on the Red Road Sobriety Walk in the summer of '92. It was a journey of forty-seven miles to the Round House that took two days by foot.

I was in charge of the medical team and drove the transport van, making sure everyone walking was okay. Occasionally I picked up those who needed a break, a drink of water, or a band-aid for blistery feet. As I drove up and down, I watched Deerfoot with his hat and walking stick. The sun beat down on the small group, and this man walked and walked, ignoring the heat. He had a fourteen year-old nephew from New Mexico. That is where Deerfoot was born.

The first day they walked twenty miles. We made camp at a site near a lake, and several women prepared a meal. Then everyone visited, sang songs and rested. Coyote, the leader, gathered us and said we would be getting up early to complete the journey to the Round House. There we would have a ceremony for all who completed the trip on foot. We were still twenty-seven miles from our destination, and much was uphill.

When we reached the Round House, I had a talk with Deerfoot and he told me about his nephew and the lessons he was learning about life. He needed the kind of guidance that only an uncle could give by example. That is our way.

At that time his wife drove to give them a ride home. I asked if he was going to stay for the ceremony.

"I would like to," he said, "but we have a new baby that needs us at home."

I said I understood. As Deerfoot was collecting his gear, his wife asked if I would like to come to their home one day. I was proud to accept the invitation. As she put it, Deerfoot did not have many friends. Then she asked if I knew how to barbeque. I said yes and we exchanged phone numbers.

As they left, I felt warm inside. It was good to meet a man committed to the walk, and most of all, to his family.

At the Round House ceremony, Coyote said the opening prayer in front of the sacred fire. He prayed for all those who walked the forty-seven miles. It took a lot of courage and strength to overcome fear, thirst and heat.

As I sat there, Coyote opened a box full of eagle feathers and called out people's names, including Deerfoot. I spoke up and said he had to leave, but I would tell him about this great gift. In the way of Native-Americans, receiving an eagle feather is among the highest of honors. I was proud of my new friend, and twelve years later, Deerfoot and I are brothers. And we're still walking the Red Road.

*Mr. Bear is a Native-American Chaplain. He and his life partner, Little Bird, live in Fresno, California. Together they have five children and twenty grandchildren.

WATCH WHAT YOU ASK FOR

By Peter J. Rondero

Dedicated to my wife, Cora; to Jerome Truppa, Sergeant Herschberger, Mike Ladich, Paul Bradford, Allan Mortenson, Tom Brown, Richard Tilghman, Andy Dupal, Ed Simonsen, Ted Johnson, Alden Mowry, Sal Lopiccolo, and all the men and women who have served our great country.

I was fifteen and my brother, Johnny was sixteen when Pearl Harbor was attacked on December 7, 1941, and the United States entered World War II. It seemed everyone was taking off to work in the defense plants. Mom made tamales and sent my brother and I door to door, selling them for five cents apiece. Johnny and I made shoe shine boxes and walked the streets earning what we could to help Mom buy food and shoes for the family. There were twelve kids.

By 1943 I was seventeen and nearing the age when I could serve my country. I wanted to be a tail gunner in a B-17, but the Army Air Force said no. The USN also said no, and the US Army said, "Hey, Kid, you're too young."

Someone told me the Marines took anyone that could walk, so I visited the recruiting Sergeant. "Here," he said. "Take these enlistment papers and have your mother sign them." I felt ten feet tall. At last I could do something meaningful with my life.

I bought Mother a box of candy and flowers and presented the enlistment papers to her to sign. She said "no!"

I cried and cried.

In time she grew tired of my sulking and finally signed the papers. On October 17th I was off to Boot Camp. I was a member of Platoon 1054. I spent three months training with fifty other boys. We were all designated as Privates and our drill instructors were Corporal Evans and Corporal Southwell. The training was rough; we were to be transformed from boys to men in ninety days. We learned to walk and march at the sound of the DI's voice. We were hollered at, did push-ups when we messed up, and ran around the parade grounds. Along with physical training, we learned military life, weapons, and Marine history. I'm glad I knew how to follow orders. I grew up obeying my parents, and if I misbehaved, I got in trouble. I got spanked, did extra work around the house, and sometimes had to kneel on rice for punishment. It prepared me for Marine life.

I met Jerome C. Truppa from San Jose, California. He and I became lifelong friends. We both graduated Boot Camp as Privates First Class. Then both of us volunteered for the Marine Raiders and trained at Camp Pendelton. This training was tougher than Boot Camp. Jerome and I were assigned to the 2nd Raider Battalion, George Company. The commanding officer was 1st/Lt. Jack Lummus, a tough Marine and fine officer.

Training consisted of physical endurance, weapons, and hand to hand combat. The most horrifying experience was making beach landings from rubber rafts. One day the company of 148 men marched to the beach. Our squad was in one of three boats facing the beach, waiting for the surface to break. Then we charged the ocean waves and went peddling from each side of the boat. We didn't time the wave right and it hit us on the front and turned us over. We all had life preservers and all we had to do was squeeze the charge and it opened up. With all the waves breaking on us, I could not touch the charge to bring me up for air. All I could see was water. I thought I was going to drown. I felt hands pulling me up and it was big Jim Wright and Red Johnson who saved my life.

The Raider Battalions were disbanded and all the men assigned to the 5th Marine Division. Along with the 3rd and 4th Marine Division, we were training for the Iwo Jima invasion. We shipped to Hawaii in 1944 and later were designated as Fox Company, 2nd Battalion, 27th Regiment, 5th Marine Division FMF. That meant more training with tanks, artillery and mortars. We practiced loading into troop transport ships, later to LST ships.

In 1945 the LSTs took us in Landing Craft Tanks to the beaches of Iwo Jima. The Second Battalion, Fox Company, was assigned Red Beach #1 for the invasion on February 19, 1945.

I was scared. This was my first baptism under combat conditions. I prayed if I got hit, that the wound would be nice and clean, where I would feel no pain. We hit the beach about nine am and all hell broke loose. Naval air planes were bombing, naval gun fire from the ships barreled over our heads. As we charged to shore I could see marines laying wounded, some gasping with deep breaths and looking pale from loss of blood. There was nothing we could do, as the Navy corpsmen were aiding the wounded and moving the dead.

We dug in near volcanic sand. It was hot and the more we dug the hotter it got. When we landed we all carried a gas mask, but they were cumbersome so most of us discarded them. Wouldn't you know it, there was an alarm sounded that there was gas in the area. I could have made a million bucks that night selling gas masks if I had any.

Death was all around us. Casualties mounted as we inched our way to conquest of Iwo Jima. I never saw the U.S. flag go up on Mount Suribachi. Our battalion was in the mid-section of the island. But I did hear all kinds of ship and vessel horns blowing. Men were hollering and singing the Marine Corps Hymn. Our platoon sergeant, Herschberger, looked through binoculars and said, "Pete, here, take a look. The Flag!" When I saw it I cried and thanked God that the battle for Iwo Jima was almost over (or so I thought).

While advancing into the Northern end of Iwo Jima, in the Kinto Point area, the ground was rocky and we could see cliffs. In front of our lines the enemy was dug in and hiding in caves. I crawled and then peered over a big boulder. I saw a Japanese soldier moving about, took aim, and fired my M1 rifle. He fell backwards. To this day I wonder if I killed him. I felt terrible but was glad that I survived another day.

On March 7, 1945, I was hit on the right side of the helmet by a Japanese sniper. The bullet ricocheted between the fiber and the steel, breaking the chin strap off and cutting my right ear in two. The impact knocked me out momentarily, then I got up, grabbed my M1 and took cover. Mike Ladich saw me covered with blood and called the Corpsman, Paul Bradford USN to dress my wounds. To this day, Mike recounts how I looked and we laugh at how close I came to being buried in Iwo Jima at the age of nineteen. Allan Mortenson remembers the bandages around my wound, and Tom Brown, the USN surgeon recalls that I was able to continue on with the troops. My wound earned me a Purple Heart Medal.

On March 24th, Lt. Richard Tilghman of the 1st platoon asked for volunteers to place air strike markers in our front lines as Fox Company was being held back and we came under heavy artillery fire. Mike Ladich, Andy Dupal, Ed Simonsen, Ted Johnson (RIP), Alden Mowry (RIP), and I stepped forward. Off we went, crawling and protecting each other from snipers. When we reached fifty yards, we spread the markers, putting rocks on them to keep the marker open so the pilots could see our lines. We waited, then returned to our lines, which by then were under fire from the Japanese. The navy planes came strafed and bombed the Japanese and it was like a 4th of July show. After it was over, the firing stopped. We then continued with the company's advance. We hadn't heard anything about our efforts until 1998, when we all received the US Navy Commendation Medal with "V" for valor, a belated (but appreciated) decoration. The Lieutenant, Richard Tilghman, retired as Senator of Pennsylvania.

Finally, on March 26, 1945, the three Marine divisions returned to Hawaii. We began training for the invasion of Japan, but President Truman ordered the Atomic bomb dropped over Hiroshima and Nagasaki, a move that probably saved over a million U.S. military personnel. On September 22, 1945 the USA forces landed on Japan for the occupation and it's all history now.

In 1946 I was discharged from the USMC, at age twenty. I met and married Cora Pasillas in 1948. Then, like a pendejo, I joined the Marine Corps Reserves at Treasure Island, San Francisco, 12th Naval District, along with Jerome Truppa. We did it to keep our WWII rank and make some extra money. Never in our minds did we expect another war.

I went to work for the Oakland Post Office in 1950, taking time off to go to summer training at Camp Pendleton, Oceanside, California. I was assigned to the 81MM Mortar section and was the squad leader. Jerome was assigned to the 60MM Mortar section. Sal Lopiccolo joined us and was assigned to a rifle platoon.

In August of 1950 the North Koreans attacked South Korea, and crossed the 38th Parallel. All Marine Reserve Units were called to active duty by President Harry S. Truman. For the next three years the USA was busy stopping the Communist North Korea and China invasion. And yes, I did my duty, along with Jerome Truppa and Sal Lopiccolo. But that's another story in itself. Maybe next time I'll be careful what I ask for.

*Peter J. Rontero retired from the US Postal Service in 1976. He and his wife, Cora, reside in Fresno, California. He is the Service Officer in the Military Order of the Purple Heart, Chapter #106, and past Senior Vice Commander in the Marine Corps League, Fresno Detachment #14. He is also an advocate for veterans in need of veterans services at the VA Hospital.

RETRACTABLE LINE

By Dick Gallagher
Dedicated to Art Cook

Have you ever wished you could take something back?

In 1960 my lovely wife, Sandy, and I bought our first house in Huntington Beach, California. We were a young, everyday couple with dreams and ambitions - and little else. But the one thing that set us apart from everyone (at least in our own minds) was the fact that we were going to have a baby. Yes, a real, live extension of ourselves. We were ready to burst. Only, it was more physically apparent on Sandy.

When we would sit outside in the cool evenings, Sandy would snuggle close and talk to me in her musical voice. One day the conversation turned to parenting. "Dick, are you going to help with the baby?"

"Oh, of course!" I assured her. "I'm taking him for walks, to the park, to ballgames, movies--"

"That's not exactly what I meant," she cut in. "I mean, are you going to help me when it's time for diaper changes."

I masked my distaste for the subject. "Oh, you know I'll help any way I can. I've seen how they fold those things and pin them in place before slipping on the rubber pants. It's a piece of cake."

"You know, Dick, I've been thinking. Up until now, laundry hasn't been a big problem. But once the baby comes I'm going to have to wash every day. We can't be going to the Laundromat all the time. I need a clothesline."

A clothesline. Now, that was a relief. All she wanted was a place to hang wet diapers. Remember, this was 1960. Few people owned automatic dryers and disposable diapers were years away from perfection.

I did some shopping. I looked in the paper and visited hardware stores before I found something suitable. I ended up buying a retractable clothesline. I bragged to my friend, Art Cook, that I had found the perfect solution to our upcoming diaper dilemma. For some reason, I liked sounding confident around Art. We talked on the phone for a half hour.

"How are you planning to put it up?" he asked.

"Oh, that's not a problem," I assured him. I bought a post to put in the ground. We'll simply pull the line and attach it to the post. It's easy."

"You know, those wet diapers can get mighty heavy," he persisted. "How are you keeping the post from moving and the line from sagging?"

"Oh, that's not a problem either," I said. The entire time I was thinking how dumb I was for not having taken it into consideration. "I'm going to put cement around the post and let it set for a day or two so it will be strong."

"How are you going to mix the cement?" was his next line.

"Oh, it's not a problem," I said.   My neighbor has a wheelbarrow and I have a shovel.

"Well, if you need any help--"

"Not a problem," I assured him. By now I'm sure he must have been getting tired of my "it's not a problem" line. "I'm sure I can take care of it."

Next day I went to the hardware store and bought a ninety pound sack of Portland cement. I dug a hole wide enough to place the post and leave plenty of space for wet cement. Next, I emptied the contents of the sack into the wheelbarrow and added water. There was nothing to it.

"Sandy," I called, when I was almost done. "Look how easy this stuff mixes. There's nothing to it."

I stuffed wet cement around the post and tamped it in place, then used a level to make sure it stood perfectly straight.

"Now we just let it set for a couple of days and we'll be ready to use it," I boasted.

The cement was dry on day three. Sandy watched while I pulled the clothesline and attached it to the post. I felt like such a handyman. Then she did something I hadn't expected. She put her weight on the line to try it. Floop! The line sagged, and the post fell on its side.

"Dick," she said, "Weren't you supposed to add sand or something?"

I hoped Art wouldn't find out that even my wife knew more about concrete than me. But as you know, nothing in marriage can be kept secret when there's humor involved. With what I learned from this experience, I should have been smart enough to invent pre-mix cement. But no, someone else invented Pampers and someone else came up with the idea of pre-mixing.

As for me, I wouldn't trade my memories of those early years of marriage for all the gold in Fort Knox.

*Dick Gallagher is retired and lives in Fresno with his wife, Sandy. He is active in the Men's Club at Holy Spirit Parish, Catholic Charities, and a number of other organizations.

ECCLESIASTES WITH MY OWN NOTES
By Evelyn E. Butler
Dedicated to my family

Ecclesiastes 3:1- 8

1. To everything there is a season, and a time to every purpose under the heaven:

2. A time to be born, and a time to die; a time to plant, and a time to pluck up that which is planted;

3. A time to kill, and a time to heal; a time to break down, and a time to build up;

4. A time to weep, and a time to laugh; a time to mourn, and a time to dance;

5. A time to cast away stones, and a time to gather stones together; a time to embrace, and a time to refrain from embracing;

6. A time to get, and a time to lose; a time to keep, and a time to cast away;

7. A time to read, and a time to sew; a time to keep silence, and a time to speak;

8. A time to love, and a time to hate; a time of war, and a time of peace.

One of my favorite quotes from the Bible is Ecclesiastes Chapter 3, verses 1 thru 8. You know it. You've heard it before.

A time to be born: yes, I was born July 19, 1922 to loving parents in a time of the 20th Century when so much would happen so fast.

A time to die: well, I haven't found a good time yet. Maybe sometime in the 21st Century, but I doubt it. I once told my kids my philosophy. "Life has been so good to me and I've enjoyed it so that, no matter how long I live, I'll still go kicking and screaming."

There have been times to kill: one of my daughters was so sensitive, she even hated to see me kill flies and spiders that invaded my home.

A time to heal: I've learned we can heal ourselves and others with faith more powerful than medicine.

A time to weep: When my oldest son was nearly killed in an auto accident and again when God called my husband home and left me alone a few years ago.

A time to laugh: nearly every day because life is so sweet.

A time to embrace: I've found that a big hug can ease a lot of hearts but sometimes we have to stand back and let things alone.

A time to keep: one of my passions is collecting memorabilia to keep my memories fresh.

And a time to cast away: Eventually it is time to pass down our possessions.

There are times to keep silent, when speaking out would only put your foot in your mouth, but sometimes your years of experience can help.

A time to love: I can't think of any time when even hate shouldn't be tempered with love.

I've lived through wars and through peace. I prefer peace, please.

*Evelyn E. Butler was born in the North West. She and her late husband enjoyed fifty-two years of marriage that produced four wonderful children. Her home now is Madera, California. She loves to write and is compiling a collection of life memories to pass on to her children and grandchildren.

SAME OLD THING
By Rebecca Romero
Dedicated to the Romero family

Every morning at our house was the same. We had to be quiet because my father worked the late shift and always slept in. My brother Andy would take the longest showers and not let anyone in the bathroom. My brother Gabriel and I watched Teenage Mutant Ninja Turtles while we waited for the first school bell to ring. The entire time, my Older sister, Victoria would still be asleep in her bed. She would stay in bed until the last possible minute.

One morning my mom was in her room ironing her clothes for work, trying not to bother Dad. I went in just to bother, when Mom asked me to wake up my sister. *All right!* I ran into the room my sister and I shared and started to jump on her bed. Being only four and rather small for my age, my jumping did not wake up my sister. She lay on her stomach. I fell to my knees and shook her, still she did not wake up. So then I tried with all my might to roll her over. Slowly I succeeded and said, "Wake up Victoria. You're going to be late."

Still nothing. Her eyes were closed and she laid still.

"Victoria!" I hollered.

Without opening her eyes she said, "I'm dead."

I drew back, my eyes wide. *My sister can't be dead. Who's going to give me a bath every day? Who am I going to follow around?* I whimpered on her white princess bed. I felt helpless, alone and scared. *How am I going to survive without my sister?*

My whimpering turned to uncontrollable sobbing. I got up and ran to my parent's room and wrapped my arms around my mother's leg. "Victoria's dead!"

My mother didn't stir like I'd expected. She just ignored my howling. I looked at my father through rivers of tears. He half-opened one eye and said, "Is she pulling that dead thing again?"

SCARECROWS ARE REAL
By Rebecca Romero
Dedicated to my brother, Gabriel

So there we were, all dressed up for Halloween. Gabriel was a pirate and I was a princess. We went from house to house with our mother, collecting as much candy as we could. Keep in mind that at that time I was only five and Gabriel was eight. As we approached one house I noticed that there was a scarecrow on the porch sitting in an old wooden chair. The scarecrow looked lifeless.

"Gabriel that scarecrow moved," I whined

"Quiet Rebecca, scarecrows are not real."

"But Gabe, I saw it move!"

Before I could say another word my mother came from behind us to see what was taking so long. Then the scarecrow jumped from his old chair and screamed. Gabriel and I stood in our same spots and watched our mother run all the way down the driveway. We never knew she could move like that. She finally came back and cursed the middle-aged man for being so mean. We didn't know she could talk like that, either. In the end I learned that scarecrows are real.

*Rebecca Romero (Becca) is a graduate of Buchanan High School. At nineteen, she loves art and Salsa dancing. She works two jobs to pay her way through college and finds time for little else. Writing is not her passion, but she loves to take a challenge.

COFFEE CAN REALLY WAKE YOU
By David Rodriguez
Dedicated to Antonio and Defina Lucero

"Hon, I need to stop up ahead and buy coffee."

"We have diet Pepsi," offered Ruth.

"It's not the same. Soda has caffeine, but coffee can <u>really</u> wake you."

It was nearing 7:00 PM. We were on our way from San Jose to Mt. Shasta, a camping trip we took every year. We dressed for comfort, sweats and tennis shoes. I pulled off the I-80 near Highway 515 and Willow. It was the last opportunity before a long, grueling drive. The sun was low on the horizon.

"I guess I could use a little snack," said Ruth, anxious to stretch her legs. We'd only been driving two hours, but it seemed longer.

I bought a large cappuccino with whipped cream and attached a plastic lid. My wife bought a bowl of soup and a large cup of strawberry ice cream. We settled in. I put my hot coffee and the ice cream in the cup holders. Ruth placed her soup on top of the cooler and held on to it..

"All right," I said. "We're ready to rumble."

I got on the frontage road and gunned the engine, picking up speed to get onto the freeway. The turn was sharp. The cup fell over and the lid came off. Thirty-two ounces of hot liquid spilled on my lap.

"Ruth!" I yelled, "this stuff is burning!" I pulled my sweats down to get the heat off my right leg. I was already on the freeway. I put my left foot on the accelerator and did the splits, stretching my right leg toward my wife.

"It's in my sock! Pull off my shoe."

I was burning. My wife held on to her soup.

"Put that soup down, will you! I need help!"

"Well stop the car," she said, yanking on my shoe.

I pulled to the shoulder and jumped out the door. My skin

166

sizzled. I yanked my sweats down to my ankles.

A trucker passed us, honking his horn. I danced in pain, leaning on the van to keep from falling.

"David, get your pants back on," hollered Ruth.

I reached in the van, grabbed my wife's ice cream, and smeared it on my leg. Pink goo ran down my thigh, over my knee, and into my sock. What a relief.

"Move your soup," I said. Flipping open the cooler lid, I grabbed a cold Diet Pepsi, shook it and popped it open. The cold soda on felt wonderful on my leg. "Ahhhhhh."

"David, please get back in the van," cried Ruth. "Everybody can see your *chonies*." Cars slowed down as they passed us. People waved. My wife covered her face.

The rest of the drive was wet and sticky. Ruth finished her soup without spilling a drop. Every once in a while, she snickered. I tried to act mad, but couldn't help laughing with her.

It's true what they say about coffee. It can really wake you up.

*David Rodriguez is a graduate of San Jose State University. He retired from the teamsters and worked as a Juvenile Group Counselor. Thirty years of marriage produced three children and one grandson, so far. His childhood can be described as Tom Sawyer-ish, and his adult life has been just as interesting.

BIG BIRD, A TEDDY BEAR, AND CHAMPAGNE
By Victoria Romero-Delsid
Dedicated to my brother, Gabriel Romero

"Can we go yet?"

My mother had just walked through the door from work and was met by my brother Andy and me, hopping up and down and repeating the question in unison. Mom carried a stack of papers in one arm, my brother, Gabriel in the other, and her purse on her shoulder. Mom's purse was huge, the style at the time. It had dozens of pockets, jammed full of papers. I thought one day she might collapse beneath its weight.

It was the day of the school carnival. My older brother, Andy and I could not contain our excitement. There were signs all over our grade school encouraging everyone's participation and I was determined to be there from the beginning until the end.

Mom sighed. "Let me change my clothes. Victoria, you change Gabriel's diaper and put clean clothes on him. Andy, you get the diaper bag together."

"But Mom, the carnival's starting! I can hear the kids." We lived across the street from the school and could hear children squealing as they played. I protested with my whole heart and my mother must have seen the desperation in my eyes.

"Oh, go ahead. I'll change the baby and we'll catch up to you later. You two stay together." She didn't even get the last of her sentence out before Andy and I were out the door.

We ran full speed through the eucalyptus trees that grew in our front yard. We jumped the chain link fence with ease and ran across the soccer field without breaking a sweat.

"Get your tickets here!" A large woman wearing a straw hat stood in front of Room 3. Her robust voice was music to my ears. I had been saving money for what seemed like forever. I beamed with pride as I reached into my pockets and spilled out five dollars in nickels, dimes and pennies onto a large table. I fidgeted as she counted every coin and handed me a fistful of bright yellow tickets.   Andy's transaction went much faster because he possessed a coveted five dollar bill. My brother could never hold on to money for long, so for him to actually have five dollars was a rare occasion.

We ran all over the carnival with the feeling of absolute joy that can only be experienced in childhood. We ate popcorn, tossed beanbags at stacks of coke bottles, and threw ping pong balls in hopes of winning goldfish. I reluctantly used my last ticket on cotton candy when I saw my mother pushing my brother in the stroller.

"Gabriel, look what I got you," I yelled as I ran to the stroller. I gave him a little rubber snake and showed my mother a plastic bracelet I had won. I rattled on about how much fun we were having.

"I think it's time for us to go home," Mom said. Her face expressed the words that she did not want to say. She had a long day at work, she had been walking around the carnival looking for us, and Gabriel had a loaded diaper.

"Aww, Mom, can't we stay just a little longer? They haven't even started the cake walk." I strained to get my eyes looking sad.

"I want you two to stay together and come home as soon as the cake walk is done. Understood?" She took her purse off her shoulder and dug through it until she produced two more five dollar bills. What luck!

"Everyone stand on a number!" Mr. Duke, our principal was the announcer. Music started and we made our way around a large circle of numbers, skipping and hopping with excitement. Suddenly, it grew quiet and everyone waited for Mr. Duke to declare the winner.

"Number 4, come over and pick out a cake." It was me! I let out a shriek and bounced all the way over to a long table filled with desserts. I picked out a cake that was decorated to look like Big Bird from Sesame Street. Then a thought occurred to me. *What am I going to do with the cake?* I couldn't very well enjoy the rest of the carnival while holding Big Bird.

I decided the best thing would be to run it home. Andy wouldn't go with me, saying it was my fault for winning. I made my way into the house through the entryway. It was an entrance that only visitors used, so I was sure I could get in undetected. By now Dad was home and I was being careful not to let anyone see me because I was only seven and I was sure they would not permit me to return to the carnival alone.

I put the cake down on the entryway floor and proceeded to sneak into the living room to see where everyone was. Mom had fallen asleep on the couch with Gabriel in her arms. I could hear Dad watering plants in the back yard. I tiptoed out and returned to the carnival.

"Number 12, come and pick out a cake." It must have been my lucky day because there I was, picking out another prize. This time I chose a large chocolate cake, shaped like a Teddy Bear with jelly beans for eyes. I ran home again and left it on the entryway floor next to Big Bird.

"Number 16, come and pick out a cake." I couldn't lose! I picked out a big pink champagne cake, thinking how my mother would love it. I just knew she'd be overjoyed because we were going to the May Day parade the following day and could take it along to snack on. This time Andy decided to go home with me because he had used up all his tickets.

We were laughing as we walked through the entryway. Then the whole thing came to a halt. To my horror, there was no more Teddy Bear and no more Big Bird. Just Gabriel with a fistful of cake. My mother awoke from her nap at the sound of my screams and Andy's exaggerated laughter.

At the parade, we ate the champagne cake, but my dad insisted it wasn't half as good as Big Bird would have been.

*Victoria Romero-Delsid is a Postal employee in Fresno, California. She and her husband, Justin, are raising two beautiful daughters. With little time for writing, she's content to read to her girls.

FROG SERENADE
By Rose Brace
Dedicated to my mom, Goldie Kelley

In the early 1970's, when I was ten years old, my mom and I went on a pilgrimage to our homeland. Mom was born and raised in the small town of McKinney, Texas. I was a city kid in need of exploring the great outdoors. It was all new territory to me.

The heat of the day gave way to afternoon shadows. I decided it was a good time to take a walk. My aunt and uncle seemed content to sit and talk with Mom, so nobody even noticed me walk out the door.

It was great to be out in the open. Weeds along the beaten path were tall and green. A butterfly landed briefly on my shoulder, then fluttered away in wild zigzags. *If only I had a jar.*

In the distance I heard the sad song of a dove. The closer I got to a thicket of trees, the more I could smell moss. It was an odor similar to wet clothes that had been left too long in the washing machine. Insects flew and buzzed on my ears. Mosquitoes landed on my bare arms and legs. I was miserable and happy at the same time. Near the water's edge I found an empty mayonnaise jar, complete with lid. *Why couldn't I have found it sooner?*

I thought of going back to look for the butterfly, when out of the corner of my eye I saw movement, followed by a splash. Goodie, there were frogs in the little swamp. I squatted down and stayed as still as the bugs allowed. The grass moved and I caught a glimpse of a fat frog. Before it could hop in the water, I pounced on it and slipped it in the jar. He stared at me through the glass with bubble eyes. I couldn't believe I had touched it, much less caught it.

Frog in hand (in jar, really), I trekked back to the house. As I approached the front door I noticed the jar contained not only a frog, but a large clump of something else too. *What happened?* I carefully unscrewed the lid to investigate. Suddenly, my captive

171

leaped out and I was left with a jar of frog poop!

Not wanting my walk to be a total loss, I screwed the lid back on the jar and took it in to show it off to the adults. Mom threw out the jar and made me take a bath.

Months later, back in California, we heard from my aunt and uncle. They wanted me to know that my frog had decided to move in under the house and raise a family. I left a lasting impression on my family in Texas. They reminded me for years of the nightly frog serenade my curiosity made possible.

*Rose Brace is the Postmaster of Cantua Creek, California. She still loves the great outdoors and is partial to frog songs.

TEMORARILY LAURA
By Connie E. Curry
Dedicated to Claire Turnbull

Have you ever wished to be someone else for just a day? Have you ever thought about how adventurous it would be to walk in on a huge wedding reception, all dressed up for the occasion and appear to be a legitimate guest? You could wine and dine for free. People probably would whisper and ask one another who you are, but no one would probably assume you were crashing the party, uninvited. Most would not have the courage to ask you, thinking they would offend Uncle John's great niece who had flown in from Rhode Island.

A similar opportunity fell into my lap. Claire, a dear friend invited me to her casual high school class reunion. We rarely find time to get together and I decided to go with her to this out of town affair, assuming I probably wouldn't know a soul.

We arrived, guests abundant and Claire immediately recognized some, and was having fun, trying to identify others after twenty-five years. I noticed classmates looking at me, inquisitive. I noticed some, whispering, pointing, and I was sure they were having discussions, trying to decide what mysterious classmate I was. They probably thought I had changed a lot in my appearance, and they would figure me out soon enough. It certainly isn't unusual to attend a reunion, after so many years, and to be unable to put a face with a name.

As I sat, watching Claire mingle among her old school friends, growing weary and feeling alone, in walked Todd, an old friend. I had not a clue this was his alumni town and his reunion, also.

"What are you doing here?" he asked me. I explained my friendship with Claire, thinking what a small world we live in, having mutual friends and discovering Claire had gone to school with him.

Later Todd approached me, "Connie, everyone's trying to figure out who you are."

"Well, give me a name. Heck, why not play along," I laughed.

"Laura Meenan," he immediately said.

"She came to our school in 1976, moved here from California and just went to school with us for two years," Todd said.

"Well, was she pretty, respectable, popular? If I am going be someone, lets make it good."

"Oh, she was hot," Todd said.

"Then, Laura Meenan it will be!" I said.

"There's Mark," Todd said, as he pointed across the room. Go mess with him, tell him you are Laura."

I walked up to Mark, a man I had never seen in my life and put my hand out to greet him.

"How are you, Mark? Remember me? I am Laura Meenan."

He studied my face as he continued shaking my hand. He held my hand, as if our touch would jog his memory. His eyebrows wrinkled and he squinted to study my face.

"Remember! We had Math class together. Mrs. Um… um…um, what was her name?" I asked, as I waited in hopes he would produce a legitimate name of a Math teacher from his school.

"Mrs. Martin! Yea, Mrs. Martin, wasn't she the tallest woman you have ever seen? I think she stood about 7 ft. tall," he reminisced aloud.

Well, if you recall, she played basketball in college. She attended college on a full ride scholarship," I said.

Claire and Todd listened, watched and they both fought laugher to prevent blowing my cover.

As someone else approached Mark, Claire mumbled to me, "Man, you are good."

"Yea, my mama would be proud of how well I lie, I thought."

"Look! Here comes Mr. Willaby, our old principal," Todd said.

We all scanned the crowd and looked beyond Todd's finger. Mr. Willaby, another strange face to me, walked toward us.

He immediately recognized Todd and Claire. They all exchanged conversation as I stood quietly watching.

"Mr. Willaby, hi…Laura Meenan, remember me?" I put my hand out to shake his.

"Laura Meenan, Laura Meenan... hmmm. Laura Meenan? Hmmm, Laura Meenan," he said, shaking my hand, as he tried to recollect who I was.

"Where did you live?" he asked.

"Hmmm. Maple Street," I said, hoping a Maple street existed in this town. (All towns have a Maple Street)

"Do you still live out off..." (I stopped; looked at Todd and so hoped he would help me out of this daring question. I realized then that I might be pushing my luck.)

I read his lips as he said, "Route 245."

"245," I said.

"Oh Lord, yes. I will die there," Mr. Willaby said.

Todd and I talked about our children as Mr. Willaby, quietly mumbled occasionally, "Laura Meenan, Laura Meenan?" He'd rub his forehead with the palm of his hand, thinking.

As my game started becoming fun and challenging, two familiar faces walked into the reunion. (My cousin and his wife.) I had totally forgotten they had graduated from this high school. I thought my false identity was about to be discovered.

"Laura Meenan, hey...remember me?"

Rick, my cousin looked at me, confused and baffled.

"Shhhh, I am Laura Meenan for the night. Don't blow my cover," I said.

They both snickered and knowing me very well as a jokester, they walked on, visiting, and talking to old school friends.

The 70's rock and roll band played on as Laura Meenan continued socializing, enjoying the evening of fooling the crowd.

"Please come to the stage for a class picture. All those from the class of 1978, please come up," blared across the band's microphone.

People slowly gathered toward the stage. I stood back, watching, thinking and grinning.

Just as everyone was standing in the appropriate places, tall ones in the back just like school days, I slithered up to the group.

It was amazing how no one seemed to notice me approach the group. I moseyed to the end of the front row, stood next to a gentleman, and smiled as the camera clicked and flashed.

Apparently the gentleman standing next to me had heard from another classmate, who I was.

"Laura Meenan, hi. Good to see you. You haven't changed a bit."

Flash went another camera.

I just smiled.

As the evening was about to end, a woman approached me.

"Could you please tell me what name I am supposed to put for you before I turn this in to the local paper? I know you are not Laura Meenan, she was in my wedding."

The game was over.

*Connie E. Curry is a Freelance Writer in Delaware, Ohio. She spends much time writing humorous nonfiction stories. In July 2001, she won the James Thurber Humor Writing Contest. Her story, WET DREAMS is a nonfiction about her son. Visit her website at http://www.geocities.com/conniescorner04.

THE FRONT WHEEL

By Timothy Avid
Dedicated to my sons, Shay and Aslan

The hill stretched long and steep in front of us. As we topped it from the back side, I felt pure joy. The grin on Dale's face told me he felt the same. There was nothing I would have rather done on a Saturday than ride bikes with my friend.

This was going to be a great ride. We got ready to plunge down the hill, side by side. I leaned and slid my five year-old body forward on my banana seat, my head almost between the high handle bars and lower than my hands. I wanted to keep up with Dale as much as possible. He was strong and fast.

Just as we started to roll, Dale popped a wheelie. I was envious because I could not get my front wheel to leave the ground unless I was going uphill. But Dale, who was two years older could do it at will. His front wheel did not just leave the ground in a short hop this time, but went high into a full wheelie. Then his front wheel dropped back to the road. Not his bike, just the front wheel! His eyes opened wide and the only thing I could think of was MOM!

I didn't see him hit the ground. I saw the wheel roll out in front of me and off to the right into the bushes. I headed down the hill as fast as I could to get help.

"Mom!" I called from the front yard. She was out of the house in a flash. We raced up the hill in the car and found my best friend, Dale. He wasn't in the middle of the street as I had thought he would be, but rather on the front porch of a nearby house. A blood soaked washcloth wrapped around his hand, he blotted the wound on his forehead.

Dale never forgave me for not stopping to help him myself. I've always wondered if it would have been better than going for Mom. I lost my best friend that day. Sometimes just stopping to stay with a friend is all the help they need.

Dale missed a whole week of school, lost his front tooth, and had a scab on his forehead for a long time. Thirty years later I still wish he would have forgiven me or that I would have stopped first, before seeking help.

*Timothy Avid is a native of the central California coast. He was born in San Luis Obispo in 1964 and grew up in Morro Bay and Atascadero. He now lives in Santa Margarita, California.

WATERMELON MARGARITAS
By Javier Lazo
Dedicated to T.C. and Lacey

Here's my recipe for watermelon margaritas, just as we made them last weekend. I also have photos of this catastrophe…you had to be there. We had a bunch of people get together in the Sierras to celebrate the second anniversary of a couple who had met and married at the site. The recipe requires a highly skilled team of professionals, including bartenders, photographers, laborers, and a medical support team. Don't try this at home.

1. Look in freezer, discover that the watermelon is frozen **whole**, not cubed as you instructed.

2. Make a batch of margaritas using prepackaged mix, one part tequila to three parts mix.

3. Drink this while you discuss with the bartending team how to cut open the frozen melon.

4. Attempt to cut melon with a large kitchen knife. Stop after nearly slicing off thumb.

5. Apply sterile dressing to bleeding thumb.

6. Attempt to cut melon with a hacksaw. Stop after nearly cutting thumb off helper.

7. Recruit a photographer who can keep from rolling on the deck laughing.

8. Attempt to use a power drill to make holes in the watermelon. Stop after nearly drilling through leg and into brand new deck.

9.   Make another batch of margaritas using pre-packaged mix, one part tequila to two parts mix because you're out of mix.

10.   Locate a five inch long pointed metal drill. Have three strong men take turns trying to shove the bar into the watermelon while holding it steady.

11.   After making a ½' hole into the still frozen watermelon (out in the sun for over an hour on a 97-degree day), stop and finish second batch of margaritas.

12.   Locate a large heavy metal bar with which to hit the five foot drill. Give precise instructions to the margarita team, "when I nod my head, hit it with the metal bar."

13.   Apply sterile dressing to head wound. *Good thing we have a nurse on hand.*

14.   Stifle the complaints of the thirsty whiners standing around by making a batch of margaritas with Jose Cuervo packaged mix. Realize after adding the mix to the tequila that JC's mix **already** had tequila in it. *Hope no one will notice.*

15.   Repeatedly pound the drill into the frozen watermelon as the team sings 'I've been working on the railroad' off key.

16.   After driving the drill three inches into the watermelon (many blows required), improvise another mix of margaritas using tequila, Triple Sec, and six limes.   Add sugar to silence the whiners who say it's too sour.

17.   Give the drill to a tall, handsome, muscular school principal of Hawaiian descent. Have him pile-drive the drill and melon into a solid concrete slab, while chanting in Hawaiian for strength.

18.   Gather the smashed pieces of melon, sorting them out from crumbled pieces of concrete slab. Carry them to the kitchen.

19. Make a batch of margaritas using one part tequila, one part Triple Sec, and piles of broken frozen watermelon. Blend. Stop blender and strain out cement grime before anyone notices.

20. Drink Watermelon Margaritas, turn on karaoke machine, and have a wonderful time.

And if it didn't happen exactly that way, it was close enough. Of the ten people present I doubt anyone could have given a more accurate description. We drank a LOT of tequila.

*Javier Lazo was born in Havana, Cuba in 1954, and grew up in Central Los Angeles. He attended the University of Notre Dame, earning a B.A. in Government. He's worked for various insurance companies in the L. A. area since 1979. He's also traveled the Central Valley extensively and been in more motel rooms than a Gideon Bible.

WHAT WAS I THINKING?

By Christine Jahn

Dedicated to my husband, Kevin and my children, Angela and Travis

One night as my family was gathered around the table for supper, my children started goofing off instead of eating. I became very aggravated and told them to eat or they would be grounded. Nobody spoke for the rest of supper and then we all went to our separate rooms. A few nights later, the same thing happened, my kids started laughing at the supper table. My son was giggling so hard that he could barely breathe and I joined him. We all ended up laughing so hard that we couldn't finish eating.

What was the difference in the outcome of these instances? My attitude. The first time, I was tired and was thinking of how I wanted them to hurry and eat so I could go relax in front of the television. The second time I was concentrating on how much I loved them and how thankful I was that we were all together. Same situation, different thought, different outcome.

So, I decided to see if this method would work with my husband also. I noticed that sometimes I had a bad attitude when he came home from work. My thoughts ran along these lines. Did he expect the house to be spotless and me to wait on him hand and foot? I was wondering what he was going to want from me. Instead of that I decided to think about what I could do for him. I happily cooked his supper and sat down to listen to him talk about his day. Believe it or not, I enjoyed the conversation that night. And it was all because I changed my expectations.

I also noticed that this "new thinking" worked when I had to go somewhere. If I looked forward to the trip, then I had a wonderful time. If I dreaded it, then I had a miserable time. As I came to realize this, I tried to change my attitude midstream to see if it changed the situation and it normally did. I would start to enjoy myself if I concentrated on having a good time.

Church was one of the places I used to love to go. Then I

noticed that I didn't look forward to it as much. I considered it to be somewhat of a chore. I decided to meditate on enjoying it, thinking that I would receive joy, peace, and love from the service. I focused on how much I loved the music and how uplifting the message was. Now I'm back on the right track to enjoying church.

When the Bible said to watch what I was thinking about, I always assumed this pertained to the obvious bad stuff like adultery, stealing, lying, and all those "awful" sins. But I now see that it also includes the little things, like concentrating on how much I love my children instead of wanting them to be quiet so I can relax. I now know that I can also be peaceful if I concentrate on enjoying them.

Do you have a relationship that needs help? Try adjusting the way you think and see what happens.

© 2002 Christine Jahn

*Christine Jahn is a freelance writer from Western Kentucky. She specializes in Christian, relationship, and/or family oriented nonfiction. She has numerous articles published in print and online in magazines and newspapers. She is a member of the National Association of Women Writers and the American Christian Writers Association. She is married with two children.
Visit Christine at http://www.christinejahn.com.

OLD BETSY

By Christine Jahn
Dedicated to Old Betsy and my childhood friend, Melissa

Old Betsy was her name. She was big, brown, and loud. She wasn't my first car but she was the first car I went cruising in. Betsy belonged to my best friend, Melissa. She got her license before me and her grandparents gave her this car. Old Betsy was our best friend.

The car had glass packs so everybody could hear us coming a mile away. The radio didn't work but we improvised by putting a jam box in the middle of us and listening to tapes. There are certain songs that still remind me of my dear friends, Old Betsy and Melissa.

Melissa and I used to joke about Betsy going through menopause. Occasionally, if we shut her off she wouldn't start back up unless we raised the hood and "fiddled with her tubes." There were some kind of wires in there that needed to be wiggled and she'd start right back up. We had no idea what they were for, but it worked.

Betsy wasn't the prettiest car out there. Some of our classmates had cool sports cars, but we didn't need that. All we needed was Betsy. She got us where we wanted to go. All our friends respected the fact that we loved that car, no matter what she looked like. We had so much fun with her.

We felt so grown up and free when we were out on the open road with Betsy. She took us on many adventures and always brought us home safely. I think Melissa's grandparents knew that if we were ever in an accident, Betsy would protect us. She was like a big tank.

One night, while on our way home from hanging out in town with our friends, we almost hit a deer. Melissa slammed on the brakes so hard I slid into the floorboard.

Back then; you didn't have to wear seatbelts. Once the initial shock was over, we were glad Betsy was ok and we laughed all the way home over our encounter with the furry creature. It didn't take much for us to have a good time.

Just recently, I saw Melissa and the first thing we talked about was Old Betsy. She's long since been retired but she'll never know how much she meant to two teenage girls and our newfound freedom on the road. Rest in peace, Betsy, you'll never be forgotten.
© Christine Jahn 2003

*Christine Jahn is a freelance writer from Western Kentucky. She specializes in Christian, relationship, and/or family oriented nonfiction. She has numerous articles published in print and online in magazines and newspapers. She is a member of the National Association of Women Writers and the American Christian Writers Association. She is married with two children.
Visit Christine at http://www.christinejahn.com.

RUNNING WITH FIRE

By Laura Gibson
Dedicated to my little Prometheus

"Is it six o'clock yet?" My five-year-old son is hopping on one foot and brandishing a straw sword, impaling imaginary bad guys next to my hip.

"Not yet. Why don't you read your sister a book, or play with your Lego's, or draw a picture while I finish getting dinner ready." This is the fifth time I've suggested such diversions to help him not watch the clock. He has an inchoate understanding of telling time; he's got the hours down but the minutes are still kind of a mystery.

"Well, when will it be six o'clock? I mean, in how many minutes? I just can't wait any more. Will you play with me?" He sits down on the kitchen floor, legs splayed out, in the way of all the preparations for our evening barbeque. It is four-thirty.

"Owen," I can hear the forced patience in my tone, "the party is over an hour away. The time will go by faster if you find something to do. You don't have to take my suggestions, you can do something else." He is quiet but doesn't move.

"How about if I just watch you." He continues to sit, his back against the sink, making motor noises and using the straw to crank his arms up and down like a marionette. A few minutes go by. I continue chopping garden tomatoes for the salad. "Now, what time is it, Mom?"

I'd like to lose my cool, turn the T.V. on, send him to his room for a few minutes of blessed quiet. I'd like to explain that this party is to entertain the families of his neighborhood friends. I'd like, for the twentieth time that day, to talk about giving people their space. Instead, I put the knife down and offer to read him a book, explaining that I will need to get back to the kitchen and finish the preparations in a few minutes.

Fifteen minutes later we have read the book and he is in the back yard catching bugs. I have asked him not to ask me about the time again. Ten minutes pass and I hear from outside the kitchen window, "Now is it six o'clock?"

And so it goes with Owen and me. I often joke that parenting has made me more and less patient than I ever thought I could be, and it's true. Owen will be six next month. Insatiable in his pursuit to understand the world, he wants to know and do it all, try everything, be involved in whatever people are doing even if he hasn't been invited. A people person, he is motivated by human interaction. Sending him to his room to be alone is the worst consequence we can deliver. "So, Mom," he often says, "what should we talk about now?" My husband and I used to worry that we had so many people circulating into our lives he would have a hard time keeping track of it all, that he would be socially exhausted and end up an introvert. But he knows everyone's names, he remembers small bits of information about them, and most days he wakes up and asks, "Who's coming over today, Mom?"

The challenge for him will be to learn how to have quiet time, to learn that not all hours are meant to be filled with other people, a lonely pursuit if you cannot survive without the constant presence of others. I need a few quiet hours to myself everyday, time to process and to reshape my perspective. When he is home he is loathe to allow this. He would love to skip the annoyance of my mandated quiet times and pack every minute with activities and entertainment, with people and noise. He is indefatigable in his pursuit of connecting with others. But I hope one of my gifts to him will be to help engender an introspective side as well. For in this increasingly complicated world, he will need to take time and process the mess that he and others will make of life.

The barbecue to celebrate the first day of summer is over. The last families just left, promising to return the favor soon. I learned something tonight about my son. I watched him lead the other children in hunting for fireflies and cicada babies, in lying on a blanket to watch for shooting stars with flashlights. At dark we brought out sparklers, something our small guests had never seen. Careful not to burn their fingers, they focused with timid joy on the fireworks in their hands. Then I lit Owen's sparkler. For the only time in the night he parted from the group and arced deep into the darkening yard shouting, "I'm RUNNING with FIRE!" with soulful glee. A speck on the edge of the yard, he ran among fireflies with his sizzling wand and squealed, and when it had extinguished he lay in the grass and gazed at the night sky, all alone.

And then he did the thing that made my heart swell, the gesture that, next to his time in the grass alone, will live in my memory from this night. He got up and asked for two more sparklers and, rather than run free, offered them to our guests and invited them to follow him skipping to the edge of the grass. Sparklers, he explained, look better in your hand if you're running. My little Prometheus, I can see him years from now, quietly processing his place in the world and then offering all of himself to it. And while his constant chatter and questioning and noise makes me crazy now, I think he does understand about looking inward better than I had imagined.

*Laura Gibson lived in the Eastern Sierra for ten years. She now lives in suburban Pennsylvania with her husband, two kids, two dogs, two fish, three frogs, and one very pesky groundhog who likes to eat her vegetables. She teaches high school English, runs and hikes, reads everything she can get her hands on, and writes--mostly fiction but some nonfiction, too.

LIGHT TROUBLE
By Teresa J. Navarette
Dedicated to my cousin, Ramona.

"Turn on the parking lights," said Ramona. It was the cool way to cruise. At the age of sixteen, there was nothing my cousin and I loved better than exercising our driving privileges on a warm San Diego evening.

"Did you see those guys checking us out?" I said.

"Maybe they were just looking at Grandpa's car." We couldn't complain. Grandpa was nice enough to let us drive his 1955 Pontiac. So what if it was older than us? In the late -1970's we weren't so picky about what we drove, as long as we could have fun.

Our evening had just begun when we saw a police officer drive by. He looked in our direction, so I waved and smiled. Next thing I knew we were being pulled over.

"Mensa!" said Ramona, under her breath. "Now look what you've done."

"I was just being friendly," I said, rolling down my window. "Shhhh, here he comes."

"Good evening officer," I said, with my sincere Colgate smile. "Is there anything wrong?"

"Let me see your driver's license and car registration, please." The cop had no expression.

I pulled out my license while Ramona fumbled through the glove compartment for the registration.

The officer pointed his flashlight at the paperwork and glanced through it. "You girls going anyplace in particular?" he asked.

"No sir, just cruising," I said. Perspiration dripped, tickling my sides. *Are we in trouble?*

"Let me tell you girls something," he said. "It's against the law to ride with just your parking lights on. Did you know that?"

Ramona and I looked at each other. *If we get a ticket Grandpa will never let us go cruising again.*

"I'm going to let you off with a warning this time," he said, "but don't let me catch you out after dark again without your headlights."

"Yes sir," we said in unison.

Whew! I turned on the headlights and watched the cop drive away.

It was not the last time we cruised Highland, nor was it the last time we drove with only the parking lights on. But it was the last time we waved at the cops.

*Teresa Navarette is Customer Relations Coordinator for the US Postal Service in Escondido, CA.

THE END

About the Author

Ben Romero was born and raised in Northern New Mexico, the fifth of seven children in an Hispanic, Catholic household. Romero is a part-time Adult Education teacher in as ESL program (English as a Second Language), and uses some of his writings as material for teaching.

He has spent the past twenty-nine years working for the US Postal Service and received a Bachelor of Arts Degree in Management with a minor in Spanish from Fresno Pacific University in 1995.

Romero is active in the Catholic church, occasionally serving as CCD Instructor, and as member of Holy Spirit Parish Men's Club. He is also a member of the Central California Hispanic Chamber of Commerce.

Romero and his wife, Evelyn, have been married thirty-three years and have five children and four grandchildren.

Dance of the Chickens: an Anthology of Light-hearted Stories is Ben's third book. His first, Chicken Beaks: Growing Up Hispanic was released late in 2003. His second book, Chicken Beaks Revisited: An Hispanic Adolescence, was released in April, 2004. Book number three of that series, Chicken Beaks Forever, deals with Hispanic migration to California and will be available in early 2005.

Visit www.benromero.com

ISBN 1-41204100-7

9 781412 041003